To Dad
Happy Christmas 2001
Love from
   Alison, Steve, Clare and Daniel
         xxx

DARLINGTON
IN THE NEWS

Lighting the skies: spectators are treated to a fabulous fireworks display at South Park.

RECORD NIGHT IN A BLAZE OF GLORY.

It was a record night in Darlington on Saturday when more than 150,000 people turned out for the annual firework spectacular. The town's South Park was packed with families for one of the region's biggest displays, which attracted record crowds and went without a hitch.

Northern Echo, 8 November 1999

DARLINGTON
IN THE NEWS

CHARLIE EMETT

First published in the United Kingdom in 2001 by
Sutton Publishing Limited exclusively for
WHSmith, Greenbridge Road, Swindon SN3 3LD

British Library Cataloguing in Publication Data
A catalogue record for this book is available from the British Library.

ISBN 0-7509-2861-1

Illustrations

Front endpaper: St Cuthbert's Church, Darlington, 1869, by Milton Drinkwater. (*Darlington Borough Council*)
Back endpaper: Throughout all the changes that have come about since this picture was taken during the 1930s one thing has remained constant – the very high standard of the *Northern Echo*. Long may this outstanding daily continue 'attacking the devil'.
Half title page: W.T. Stead, editor of the *Northern Echo* from 1871 until 1880, one of the greatest names in journalism.
Title page: Bank Top Station, Darlington.

Typeset in 11/14pt Photina and produced by
Sutton Publishing Limited, Phoenix Mill,
Thrupp, Stroud, Gloucestershire GL5 2BU.
Printed and bound in England by
J.H. Haynes & Co. Ltd, Sparkford.

Contents

INTRODUCTION   11

FIRST WORLD WAR AND ALL THAT JAZZ   17

'DON'T GO DOWN THE MINE DADDY'   35

'THERE'S A WAR ON'   57

'THERE'S A PEACE ON'   73

THE OLD ORDER CHANGETH   89

THE PROGRESSIVE YEARS   105

A CHANGING ENVIRONMENT   111

ACKNOWLEDGEMENTS & PICTURE CREDITS   125

What fashion-conscious ladies were wearing during the Edwardian era, 1901–10. Recreating the vogues seen during the early years of the *Northern Echo* are Amy Swainston (three) with her sister Katherine (fifteen, standing left) and mum Lesley (standing right). They model Victorian and Edwardian costumes while Claire Swainston (nineteen) wears a replica of one of Queen Victoria's dresses. This picture was taken in 1986.

Introduction

It was the development of a national railway system following the opening of the Stockton & Darlington Railway that persuaded John Hyslop Bell to found a newspaper in Darlington. It was to be called the *Northern Echo* and would sell for just a halfpenny, making it available to everybody – of that he was adamant. It was to be printed in Darlington and copies would be on sale in cities as far apart as London and Edinburgh on the morning following publication. Hyslop Bell's timing was good because that year, 1870, Forster's Education Act became law. It would bring into being a new generation of educated working-class people; prior to 1870, two-thirds of the country's working class were unable to read. Hyslop Bell headed a group of far-sighted northern businessmen, all determined to 'supply a want of the age and district' through a well-conducted, high-class daily newspaper advocating liberal opinions and published at a price that would bring it within reach of all classes.

In 1871, the *Northern Echo*'s first editor, W.T. Stead, was appointed. This outstanding journalist, who was said to have printer's ink in his veins, stayed with the paper until 1880 before moving on to become the most famous journalist of his day.

The *Northern Echo*'s first home was a modest terrace in Priestgate and from the outset it was very popular. Stead's articles were perused by readers throughout the country, and on one memorable occasion the Prime Minister, W.E. Gladstone, told him: 'To read the *Echo* is to dispense with the necessity of reading other papers. It is admirably got up in every way.' The *Northern Echo* was founded as a Liberal, Nonconformist and Free Trade paper.

When, in 1895, E.D. Walker became its sole proprietor, he modernised production methods, installed new presses and enlarged the paper. Then, in 1903, he sold it to the newly formed North of England Newspaper Co. Ltd, which was backed by the Joseph Rowntree Service Trust. The chairman

W.T. Stead regularly tethered his dogs and pony to this piece of granite, sited outside Darlington's Public Library, while he went about his duties as editor of the *Northern Echo*.

The development of a national railway system, following the opening of the Stockton & Darlington Railway on 27 September 1825, was a contributory factor in the decision to establish the *Northern Echo* in Darlington in 1871.

of the company was Arnold S. Rowntree and the manager was Charles W. Starmer. Under their control the *Northern Echo* became the foremost newspaper in the region.

As the *Northern Echo* developed, so did Darlington. It became known as a newspaper town because it was the only place in England to publish and distribute a daily paper with a circulation far in excess of its population. In March 1867, Darlington got its first charter and the first elections to the local authority were held in December that year. In the 1868 General Election, Edmund Backhouse, a Quaker, became Darlington's first MP. In 1915, Darlington acquired county borough status and today has twelve wards.

Also in 1915, the *Northern Echo*'s prestigious new home at the corner of Crown Street and Priestgate was opened. In September 1914, the *Northern Echo*'s sister paper, the *Northern Despatch* had been launched; and now, from their spanking new headquarters, both newspapers covered the First World War and other news, whenever possible with local slant. If it was newsworthy, the newspapers belonging to the North of England Newspaper Co. Ltd reported it, applying the same high standard of care and accuracy to local events as to world news. This is what the readership wanted and came to expect.

During the 1920s and 1930s, many Darlington folk reacted against the horrors of the First World War by adopting a hedonistic lifestyle and looking forward to what they hoped would be a rosy future. Others were reduced to selling matches on street corners.

It was a time when many Darlingtonians were employed by the LNER and Bank Top station was an important stop on the East Coast main-line route from King's Cross, London, to Scotland. But the railway connection went deeper than that. The LNER locomotives were built at North Road Railway Workshops, so Darlington also became known as a railway town.

During the 1920s and 1930s, Darlington was much involved in heavy engineering. Whessoe Ltd – established in 1790 as an ironmonger's shop in Tubwell Row by William Kitching, a Quaker – developed so quickly that by the 1920s it had become a huge company, supplying every type of engineering product from castings for the railways to capital equipment for the gas, oil and petro-chemical industries.

During the Second World War, Whessoe produced all-welded tank hulls for Churchill tanks and bombs of all types. Darlington could never be called a shipbuilding town, yet Whessoe also built nearly 100 types of vessel, including tank landing craft, gunboats, rocket ships and frigates, and dredger pontoons. These were prefabricated and taken to shipyards on the River Tees where they were assembled and fitted out. During the postwar years, Whessoe became Darlington's largest employer; it was at the forefront of the nuclear power industry for which it constructed pressure vessels.

An empty Northgate, Darlington, in 1864, six years before the *Northern Echo* became established in nearby Priestgate.

Skating on Hundens' Pond in 1935. This was a popular leisure activity.

From its base off Neasham Road, the Cleveland Bridge and Engineering Co. Ltd built bridges throughout the world, including the world's longest single-span example over the River Humber. As part of a consortium, it helped construct the Thames Barrier.

In their day, other industries thrived in Darlington alongside heavy engineering: Paton and Baldwins, the wool people, and Rothmans, the cigarette manufacturers, among others. Whatever its style, Darlington was growing and its citizens had a thirst for information. The *Northern Echo* and the *Northern Despatch*, an evening publication, considered it their bounden duty to satiate that thirst.

When Sir Charles Starmer became director of North of England Newspapers, the group gained the benefit of what turned out to be the brightest business brain in its entire history. He was a shrewd financier who was an organiser rather than a communicator. He had a lot of circulation-boosting ideas for his other papers in other parts of the country and used the *Northern Echo* as a means of testing them out. He wanted a loyal readership and believed that the best way to achieve this was to make *Echo* readers feel that they were part of a large and happy family.

In 1920, the *Northern Echo*'s fiftieth anniversary was celebrated in fine style with 660 couples who were celebrating their silver wedding anniversaries receiving inscribed

Floodlit St Cuthbert's, Darlington's
parish church.

silver-plated teapots and many others also getting presents. Children born on 1 January 1920 were awarded savings certificates and pensioners also received gifts. The great give-away was a huge success, as Sir Charles Starmer had foreseen.

In 1926, a General Strike was staged throughout Britain in sympathy with the miners who were refused employment by the colliery owners except at reduced rates. The *Northern Echo* did not take sides; both parties in the dispute had clear faults and it recognised this fact. Even so, the paper was wrongly accused of employing non-union labour. Both sides in the dispute eyed the *Northern Echo* with suspicion. Pickets in Priestgate caused ugly scenes and road haulage costs for delivering the papers soared. It would have been easier and cheaper to close the paper but that would have been unethical, so the *Northern Echo* remained in business and gained the respect of its readers.

For the 1927 eclipse of the sun, the *Northern Echo* hired a plane so that its reporters could get a closer look. From the ground, people could see little because of low cloud. But the *Echo* aircraft was always in view of the sun and could be heard overhead. It was a brilliant publicity stunt, one of a great many that would take place over the next few years, the best of which generated mass involvement. On Monday 21 October 1929, the Nig Nog Club, another of Sir Charles Starmer's brilliant ideas, was started. Uncle Mac,

Derek McCulloch of BBC *Children's Hour*, hosted it. From the outset it was a great success. On 12 November 1929, the first young reader was enrolled in the Nig Nog Club and by 30 January 1930, 50,000 youngsters had signed up. Nig and Nog lived on the moon and one of their jobs was to keep the man in the moon awake. They also raised cash so that they could send unhealthy or poor children to a guest house near Scarborough for a holiday.

By 1934 the *Northern Echo* was selling 100,000 copies a day. Its readership had now spread far beyond its South Durham heartland to Berwick in the north and York to the south. During the dark years of the Second World War, plans were drawn up to transfer production to Durham City should Priestgate be bombed and on two occasions in 1941 the *Northern Echo* was printed outside Priestgate.

Following the declaration of peace, the *Northern Echo* retained its 1920s outlook and seemed in danger of becoming a nonentity. Then, in 1961, Lancastrian Harold Evans, later of *The Sunday Times*, became its editor. He likened the paper to an empty rocket: 'All I had to do was put some fuel in the engine', he said, 'and nobody had done that for some time.' The effect was magical. The *Northern Echo* took off and within five and a half years was regarded with respect and admiration in the highest journalistic circles. Nothing like this had happened since Stead's day. It remains a high-flyer today, thanks to the brilliant editors who followed the lead Evans had given. And a high-flyer the *Northern Echo* will rightly remain, as long as there are enlightened editors like Peter Barron, currently occupying Stead's famous chair, to steer it along a clear course into the future.

W.T. Stead's chair has pride of place in Darlington's *Northern Echo* offices.

First World War and all that Jazz

On Monday 2 September 1907 the New Hippodrome and Palace of Varieties was formally opened under the management of Rino Pepi and it thrived. This is an excerpt from its first programme:

Tonight: Twice nightly. Starring engagement at tremendous cost of Miss Marie Loftus, the Greatest of all Comediennes . . . Charlie Williams, the Scotch Nigger. Mezetti and Mora, comedy triple bar performers. Eight Phydoras in their Eccentric Comedy Musical Act. Morny Cash, The Lancashire Lad. Vandinoff, who paints beautiful pictures in a remarkably short time. Mdlle Lumiere's New Electrical Fairy Grotto. The Most Charming and Beautiful Act on earth.

Popular prices: Gallery 2*d*: Pitt 4*d*: Orchestra Stall 6*d*: Grand Circle 1*s*: Children 6*d*: Box to hold four 10*s* 6*d*: single or extra seats 2*s*.

BOX OFFICE AT THE HIPPODROME 11–4.

Northern Echo, 3 September 1907

Ignatius Timothy Trebitsch Lincoln, a Hungarian Jew, was born in 1879. He was Liberal MP for Darlington from January to December 1910, having defeated Herbert Pike Pease, a Unionist, by 29 votes in a turnout of 95 per cent of all the male voters. The Liberals were strong in north Darlington, and one of them, an engine driver called Tommy Crooks used to stop his locomotive outside a signal-box and argue politics with a Tory signalman. The Conservatives and Unionists were very strong in west Darlington and around Peases Mill. In Darlington, at that time, red was the Conservative colour, and before elections mill girls wore red bloomers in honour of Pike Pease. MPs were unpaid and Lincoln was a spendthrift, so he launched a scheme for taking over oil wells in Southern Poland. He borrowed from many Darlington Liberals, Tommy Crooks alone refusing to lend anything. When the bankers who were to put up most of the money backed down, his Darlington creditors began to ask for their money back. Lincoln found himself on the verge of bankruptcy.

In 1914, penniless, Lincoln made contact with a German consul in Holland and early in the war was reported to be working for Germany. He went to America, but was brought back to England on a charge of forgery. He was released in 1919 from a three-year sentence and went to Germany where he plotted for the restoration of the monarchy, but was forced to flee the country. In 1926, he went to China, but fearing treachery, retired to a Buddist monastery in Ceylon. He returned to England to see his son before his execution for murder, but arrived too late and was last reported broadcasting for the Japanese from secret radio stations in Tibet.

Northern Echo, 11 October 1943

The White Star liner *Titanic*, then the largest vessel afloat (about 45,000 tons), collided with an iceberg on the night of 14 April 1912 on her maiden voyage from Liverpool to New York. Altogether, 1,490 lives were lost, only 711 survivors being picked up by the *Carpathia*.

Civilised communities . . . were stunned by today's news that the White Star liner *Titanic* had collided with an iceberg and was sinking 600 miles off Nova Scotia. For nearly twelve hours (the Company's offices) had no news save the first wireless intimation sent by the Marconi operator on board the *Titanic*. It was couched in vivid phrase without circumlocution: 'Have struck an iceberg 41°–46" North, 50°–14" West. Am badly damaged. Rush Aid.

Northern Echo, 16 April 1912

For the *Northern Echo* the story was particularly poignant: one of the passengers lost was W.T. Stead, the paper's first editor. This picture is from the *Illustrated London News*.

Patriotic Darlingtonians volunteering to serve as a Darlington 'Pals' Company in the Kitchener Regiment which Colonel Burdon is raising for County Durham. Colonel Walker said the trenches were unbelievably crude. 'Life went on at a very low level but the Durham men were generally better than others at making trenches habitable and dry because of their pit experience. I remember one man from Wolsingham,' Colonel Walker reminisced, 'digging a mate out after he had been buried. He got his head clear and they were talking and smoking a cigarette as the rescue continued. Then the Germans lobbed over another shell which covered the man up again. The Wolsingham chap yelled over the lines: 'Hold on, Jerry, until I can get this lad out.'

Northern Echo, undated, 'memory lane'

The Ypres salient saw almost continous fighting throughout the First World War: first battle 19 October–22 November 1914; second battle 22 April–25 May 1915; third battle, also called Passchendaele, 31 July– 6 November 1917. But courage is not confined to major battles. Private Thomas Kenny of 13th Battalion, The Durham Light Infantry won his Victoria Cross between major battles near La Houssoir on 4 November 1915.

Private
Thomas Kenny, V.C.
13th Battalion, The Durham Light Infantry
1915
France.

For most conspicuous bravery and devotion to duty on the night of 4th November, 1915, near La Houssoie.

When on patrol in a thick fog with Lieutenant Brown, 13th Bn. Durham Light Infantry, some Germans who were lying out in a ditch in front of their parapet, opened fire and shot Lieutenant Brown through both thighs. Private Kenny, although heavily and repeatedly fired upon, crawled about for more than an hour with his wounded officer on his back, trying to find his way through the fog to our trenches. He refused more than once to go on alone, although told by Lieutenant Brown to do so. At last, when utterly exhausted, he came to a ditch which he recognised, placed Lieutenant Brown in it, and went to look for help. He found an officer and a few men of his battalion at a listening post, and after guiding them back, with their assistance, Lieutenant Brown was brought in, although the Germans again opened heavy fire with rifles and machine guns, and threw bombs at 30 yards distance. Private Kenny's pluck, endurance and devotion to duty were beyond praise.

Opposite: It was the early days of tanks and four had been detailed for the first trial. The first one to go got stuck in a great mass of mud. To one side there were some railway sleepers. I could dimly see four men in their great-coats, watching. 'Come on you fellows: get a move on and carry them over there.' Soon we had a solid surface for the other tanks to move safely over. Presently a Sergeant came to me and said, 'You are wanted in that dug-out, sir.' I went down to the dugout and saw four officers, a major-general, a brigadier and two colonels. 'This is your fatigue party, sergeant-major.' I nearly fell through the floor.

G.F. Bennett (Captain ret'd.), Chilton Hall, Ferryhill, *Northern Echo*, 17 March 1964
(readers' personal experiences of the 1914–18 war)

These Darlington girls worked in a shell shop in 1916. Surely Canon Lillingstone can't have had them in mind when he spoke of women who seemed to have forgotten their men at the front.

CANON SPEAKS OUT

A remarkable address was given yesterday at St Cuthbert's Hall, Darlington, by Canon Lillingstone of Durham. 'Immorality', he declared, 'occupies a very big place in the minds of people today . . . In pit villages', he added, 'the women whose husbands were at war were not acting faithfully and some of the clergy hardly knew what to do'. The women almost defended their conduct when approached about it. The other day a clergyman spoke to some of them, and they did not seem to see any harm in what they did.

Northern Echo, 7 April 1916

The First World War, 'the war to end wars', was fought so that children like these could live in peace. It was an ideal that became unattainable.

END OF THE WAR

Germany surrenders. Armistice signed. Press Bureau, Monday 10.20 a.m.

The Prime Minister makes the following announcement: The armistice was signed at 11 o'clock this morning and hostilities are to cease on all fronts at 11 a.m. today. The following wireless news was transmitted through the wireless stations of the French Government yesterday: Marshal Foch to Commanders-in-Chief: Hostilities will cease on the whole front as from 11 November at 11 o'clock (French time).

Northern Echo, 12 November 1918

To a great many people the 1920s were a time of glamour and sophistication, a time when women broke free from uncomfortable Edwardian corsets into drop-waisted dresses. It was a time of flapper fashion, silent movies and the Charlestone. Women cut their hair short, went to cocktail parties and smoked cigarettes from long holders. Men wore gangster-style suits and hats with brogue shoes. This was 'easy street', but at the bottom of the pile was 'skid row'.

The Royal Agricultural Show, Darlington, 1920 plays host to HRH the Duke of York. '*Royal Show, Darlington*. 29 June–4 July 1920. The Duke of York at the Royal Show chatting with the Marchioness of Londonderry, with the Marquess of Londonderry.' The Duke of York also inspected a guard of honour, 1st Battalion Prince of Wales own (West Yorkshire Regiment) in Darlington and was escorted around the Showground by the Mayor of Darlington and Lord Londonderry.

Northern Echo, 1 July 1920

It isn't fair! August Bank Holiday and everybody's gone to Redcar except me. I'm in Tubwell Row. That's Clapham's rope works behind me. Sunshine, showers and smiles – a bank holiday like those of the good old pre-war days.

CRAMMED SEASIDE RESORTS

Merry scenes on the sands of the East coast. The August bank holiday has really come into its own again. Everyone seems to agree that yesterday's record surpassed those set up in happy, inexpensive pre-war days.

15,000 Trippers at Redcar. For the greater part of the day the weather was fine as Redcar, though dull, with a strong wind blowing. In the evening rain fell smartly.

Northern Echo, 2 August 1921

Opposite: Not everyone went to the seaside for their holidays. Some stayed at home and played tennis. Like the enthusiast who, every hour on the hour, asked if anyone would play against him, but to no avail. Undaunted, as 10 p.m. approached he asked again, 'Anyone for tennish?'

The Duke and Duchess of
York at Darlington on
27 September 1925 for the
centenary celebrations of the
Stockton & Darlington
Railway. The idea for the
celebration originated with
the Manchester and
Liverpool railway workers
and it was entirely organised
and planned by them.

The Duchess of York (centre) inspecting locomotives participating in the centenary Railway Cavalcade at Darlington, 27 September 1925.

All controversy in the railway world was forgotten when the railway companies and three railway trade unions joined together harmoniously and enthusiastically to celebrate the centenary of the railways on the actual date of the opening of the Stockton & Darlington track on which the first railway passenger train was ran.

Northern Echo, 28 September 1925

The Duke of York (second from the left) and the Duchess of York (fourth from the left) visiting Darlington for the centenary celebrations of the Stockton & Darlington Railway. Third from the left is Sir Nigel Gresley, designer of many famous locomotives.

This plaque commemorates the laying of the first rail of the Stockton & Darlington Railway. Thomas Meynell, JP of Yarm, one of the promoters of the railway and its first chairman, officially laid the line's first rail on 23 May 1822.

CENTENARY EXHIBITS
Stockton and Darlington Collection: In connection with the commemoration of the centenary of the opening of the Stockton and Darlington Railway a special exhibition has been formed in the Science Museum, South Kensington, as a supplement to the general railway groups of the land transport collection.
Northern Echo,
28 September 1925

At first only the king and the royal household in England used seals, but by the early thirteenth century ownership of a seal was not uncommon. The railway companies sealed their documents with 'wafer' seals. Documents bearing them were on display at the Railway Pageant at Manchester to celebrate the centenary of the Stockton & Darlington Railway.

CELEBRATIONS
With the co-operation of all railway groups and all the railwaymen's trade unions, the Centenary Celebrations took place in Belle Vue Gardens, Manchester, yesterday, on the actual day of the opening of the Stockton and Darlington track over which a passenger train was run 100 years ago.
Northern Echo, 28 September 1925

It was shareholders, many of them Darlington and Stockton Quaker businessmen prepared to risk their cash, who enabled the newly developing railway system to expand.

Trying to get in on the transport act the Cleveland Car Co. Ltd, Darlington, placed advertisements in the *Northern Echo*. Motoring was still in its infancy and charabanc passengers had little protection from the weather. But it was a start: the automobile had come to stay.

TELEPHONE 369.   TELEGRAMS "AUTOMOBILE, DARLINGTON"

Cleveland Car Co., Ltd., Darlington.
▲▲▲

Motor Outings of Any Distance Quoted for.

Open Cars, Limousines and Landaulettes for Hire.

The above CHAR-A-BANC will run, weather and circumstances permitting, on

To   Return Fare

Starting from

Seating accommodation for **18** *Passengers.*

It is to be understood that this Motor does not run unless there are 14 or more passengers.

There had been a horse market in Bondgate, Darlington, for as long as these 1920 horse traders could remember. True, times were changing and now newfangled, electric-powered trams ran along Bondgate, but the horse was still king. Yes, horses had to be fed and watered whether they worked or not and some could be temperamental, but they were reliable and could go almost anywhere. Their movements were not restricted by tram lines.

When the cattle mart was ear-marked for closure a meeting was held at the King's Head Hotel, Darlington, to enable interested parties to find out what the future held. Zissler's butchers were there.

BANK TOP MART

New Company to open Darlington Premises. Old one to close. There was a large attendance at a meeting at the Kings's Head Hotel, Darlington, yesterday for the purpose of placing before farmers, butchers and others interested particulars of a new company to be known as the Darlington Farmers Auction Mart and which will carry out business at the Bank Top Mart.

Northern Echo, 1 December 1925

Opposite, bottom: A locomotive's cab, the real driving force behind all rail travel.

CHEAPER 'SEASONS', LNER COMPANY TO ISSUE WEEKLY CONTRACTS

The LNER announce that between certain stations these new tickets will enable holders to travel when they like, as often as they like and by any train they like. The new proposals are an extension of a facility which is already offered by the LNER on other parts of the system.

Northern Echo, 2 December 1925

This is Victoria Road, a quiet street in the 1920s. The far end of Victoria Road is the back entrance to Bank Top railway station and to the right of the clock tower is Darlington Farmers Auction Mart, which was featured in the newspaper report opposite.

There was a white Christmas in 1925.

AN OLD-FASHIONED CHRISTMAS

Seasonable Weather For The North Predicted. Havoc of the Storm. Railways Ready For a Record Holiday Rush Today. Eveything points to this Christmas being a good old-fashioned 'white' one – in the North at any rate, where further falls of snow are predicted. The storms of the last two days have caused incalculable damage both in this country and abroad. Telegraph and telephone services were disorganised and with trains running late many people will receive their parcels late. The railways are prepared for an extraordinary rush of holiday makers today. Main line trains are to be run in duplicate. The parcels traffic on the LNER is the heaviest for years.

Northern Echo, 24 December 1925

Throughout the North-East, people set about welcoming the New Year in the time-honoured way while the *Northern Echo* reported a new slant to the festive season.

FATHER TIME'S LEG PULLED

A New Year's Eve Wireless Prank. In addition to the special New Year greetings and services which are to be broadcast, it is hoped that there will be greetings from America, relayed through Keston. The opportunities that will be offered are as follows: 1) Dance this year to this year's dance music. 2) Dance this year to music actually being played next year. 3) Dance next year to music actually being played this year. 4) Dance next year to next year's dance music.

Northern Echo, 31 December 1925

'Don't go Down the Mine, Daddy'

As 1926 grew older, it became increasingly clear that all was not well in the coalfields. Feelings were running high on both sides.

NO SETTLEMENT: COAL WAR

Mines Stoppage From Midnight. Nation's Grave Hour. TUC Threatens To Call Out All Labour. At 11.15 o'clock last night it was officially announced that there was no settlement in the coal crisis . . .

Northern Echo, 1 May 1926

By 3 May 1926 the industrial relations situation had deteriorated to such an extent that the government was obliged to send an ultimatum to the TUC.

GOVERNMENT ULTIMATUM TO THE TUC

Unconditional Withdrawal Of The General Strike Demand. No Negotiations While State Is Threatened. The Prime Minister has issued the following message to the Nation: 'Keep steady! Remember that peace on earth comes to men of good will'. Traders That May Cease Work: Transport (sea, rail and road): Printing Trade (including the Press): Iron and Steel Trades: Heavy Chemical Groups: Building Trade (except housing): Electricity and Gas (for power).

Northern Echo, 3 May 1926

COAL SETTLEMENT STANDSTILL

The Nation is in dire straits: great diplomacy is needed to save the day. Nation Awaits Prime Minister's Statement in Commons. Northern Moves. Desire In Northumberland and Durham to Resume Talks. The Nation is bleeding industrially at every pore but still there is no official move towards a settlement of the disastrous coal mining stoppage. Reports of industrial concerns closing down are all too frequent. Parliament resumes tomorrow and the Prime Minister will have an opportunity to restate the Government's policy. He has said nothing on the question since the letters to the owners and the miners a week ago when he warned them that his offer of a subsidy of £3,600,000 to ease the settlement would expire tonight at midnight, and would not be renewed.

Northern Echo, 31 May 1926

Even the *Northern Echo* camera competition winners were affected by the strike because the country was at a standstill. May as well be philosophical about it. The Punch Bowl, Blackwell, Darlington kept a good brew. Fancy a jar?

NORTHERN ECHO CAMERA COMPETITION

Owing to the General Strike, delay has been occasioned in sending out the cameras to those readers who have qualified in the above competition. Every effort is being made, however, to have the cameras despatched at the earliest possible moment.

Northern Echo, 31 May 1926

SHOWERY WEATHER FOR THE FIRST TEST

Can England Bowlers win Game on Soft Wicket? Not a spare Bed in Nottingham. The British Empire will be agog with excitement today when the first Test Match between England and Australia opens at Nottingham. The weather forecast is showery and the problem at once arises: Can England with a bowling side picked to do execution on a hard wicket tumble Australia out on a sticky pitch? G.A. Faulkner, the *Northern Echo* special correspondent, thinks that unless something sensational happens today, the probable result is a draw. Everything may depend on Tate and Roots.

Northern Echo, 16 June 1926

Darlington awaited the Prime Minister's statement about the mining industry in June 1926.

EIGHT-HOUR DAY FOR MINERS

Government To Introduce A Bill Immediately. No Wage Reductions In Many Areas. In the Commons last night the Prime Minister said that the Government has decided on a longer day for the coal industry. It will introduce legislation to enable eight hours to be worked during a certain period. He had received positive assurances from the owners that on the basis of an eight-hour day there are certain districts producing about half the output of the Country in which the men would be offered existing wages. For the rest of the country the reduction asked would be materially less than 10 per cent. A Bill to give the reoganisation proposals of the Coal Administration is to be introduced. The £3,600,000 subsidy would be spent in assisting to meet the needs of the miners displaced from the pits.

Northern Echo, 16 June 1926

FASHION

During the 1920s women who had worked during the war found new financial and social independence. They wore skimpy, drop-waisted dresses stitched with pearls and crystals. They cut their hair short, wore make-up and smoked in public. Restrictive corsets were replaced by cylindrical underwear that flattened the chest and had suspenders attached to hold up stockings. Many dispensed with their petticoats; and dresses like those pictured here were out. By 1926 hair styles had become very boyish with the Eton Crop. Indeed, 1920s vogue was turning girls into boys.

The *Northern Echo* was quick to respond to the needs of poor children with its Shilling Fund. If it is a shilling, it will do. It may be ancient, double-headed or a spanking new one ahead of its time, all of which are pictured here.

1,000 MORE DISTRIBUTED

The steady response to the *Northern Echo* Shilling Fund appeal during the past few days made it possible yesterday to allocate a further 1,000 shillings for the relief of necessitous children in ten distressed districts. The total amount distributed so far is 11,160 shillings.

Northern Echo, 1 July 1926

TO THE BEST ADVANTAGE

Middleton in Teesdale has both helped the fund and been helped from it. Acknowledging receipt of the cheque for 60 shillings sent to him, Mr H.W. Tustin of 9 Hill Terrace, Middleton-in-Teesdale gives further testimony of the fine spirit which prevails in that town. He writes: 'I beg to thank you for the letter and for the cheque for 60 shillings which I shall use to the best advantage of the necessitous children in this district'.

Northern Echo, 1 July 1926

Darlington Railway Disaster. The Overturned Engine of the Train.

An inscription in Hetton Le Hole cemetery on a headstone marking the grave of a victim of the 1928 Darlington Railway Disaster reads 'accidentally killed'. Fifteen of those who died were members of Hetton Mothers' Union on their annual outing to Scarborough.

EIGHT DEAD IN RAILWAY DISASTER AT DARLINGTON

Tyneside Excursion and Goods Train In Midnight Collision. 2 Packed Coaches Telescoped At Entrance to Bank Top Station. About 30 Injured. Harrowing Rescue Scenes By Lamp Light. A terrible railway accident occurred just before midnight last night outside Darlington Bank Top Station. *Stop Press.* 22 Dead.

Northern Echo, 28 June 1928

The *Northern Echo* Nig Nog Club badge which was found with a metal detector by Sydney Cooper from Marton.

THE NIG NOG POST BAG

A Rush To Join The Children's Ring. I am feeing greatly pleased with myself. And why? Simply because my expectations have been realised. You remember the Nig Nog membership coupon appeared in the *Northern Echo* last Saturday. This coupon provided the opportunity for my nieces and nephews to join the Children's Ring and become 'Nignogs'. What a splendid response there has been! In fact, to use a well-known phrase, I am literally 'snowed under' with letters – letters – letters, all containing coupons, coupons, coupons . . . Several of my Nignog nieces, and nephews when sending their coupons have asked if their brothers and sisters can become members, I say 'yes, by all means. Get them to fill up the coupon. I'll do the rest'. Uncle Mac.

Northern Echo, 12 November 1929

DARLINGTON ON A STAMP

Old Darlington In Stamps. St Cuthbert's church, Darlington, and old shops, which at one time occupied sites in the Market Place, [have appeared] on postage stamps for which Mr V.W. Heslop of Messrs. Heslop and Son was awarded second prize in a national competition.

Northern Despatch, 18 September 1930

In 1932 'on yer bike' had no political connotations.

CYCLING FEAT FIFTY YEARS AGO

Darlington Man's Achievement On Cinder Track. The jubilee of a remarkable cycling achievement in the days of the 'penny farthing' machines is being quietly celebrated this week by Mr Alec Crombie, a popular Darlington personality of 71 High Northgate. Fifty years ago – 14 October 1938 to be precise – Mr Crombie won the ten miles cycle championship of Darlington and the one mile bicycle handicap and he has two gold medals to commemorate the event. The venue of the races was Johnson's Cycling and Recreation Ground, a cinder track situated on the south side of Crown Street, Darlington.

Darlington & Stockton Times, 15 October 1982

During the 1920s Art Deco, which often featured Aztec and Egyptian styles, played a prominent role. It was the most important design movement of the 1920s and the forerunner of modernism in the 1930s. The new popularity of sporting and outdoor activities emphasised slim figures for both men and women and advertising posters reflected the trend, as this one shows. Sports stars were becoming as glamorous as film stars and fashion reflected this. Until stars like French tennis champion Suzanne Lenglen appeared on the scene women had always worn everyday clothes for tennis. Now all that would change.

The home of the
news, 1930s.

During the Great Depression of the 1930s manufacturers had to advertise their wares and compete for business as never before. In the General Strike of 1926 the country came to a standstill for nine days. Young socialites drove ambulances, buses and trams because it was great fun, but by the end of the 1920s those same people had more sympathy for the workers. After the Wall Street Crash of 1929, the repercussions in Europe were far reaching and dramatic. Extreme political movements emerged led by Benito Mussolini (1883–1949) in Italy, Francisco Franco (1892–1975) in Spain and Adolf Hitler (1889–1945) in Germany. A few wealthy individuals still enjoyed an endless round of parties, but most people were suffering during the country's most serious economic crisis. Unemployment was high and political movements and trade unions were struggling for more power.

The pool at Baths Hall can be covered to become a ballroom. At the Darlington Press Ball everyone was in the swim – literally if the floor collapsed!

DARLINGTON PRESS BALL. THE ARTISTS WHO WILL PROVIDE THE CABARET

Tickets are selling rapidly for the fifth annual Darlington Press Ball to be held in the Baths Hall on Tuesday, March 13th, in aid of journalists' charities. Each year the demand for tickets increases but, as on previous occasions, the number to be issued will be limited. Jack Marwood and his Band, of Stockton, and Bobby Dixon and his Band, of Durham, who will supply the music for the non-stop dancing, are busy preparing the programme of the latest hits. In some numbers the two bands, each of ten musicians, will play in unison. The cabaret is to be given by members of the Du Barry Company who will be at the New Hippodrome next week.

Darlington & Stockton Times, 24 February 1934

King George V was born in 1865, became king in 1910 and died on 20 January 1936.

FUNERAL OF KING GEORGE AT WINDSOR ON TUESDAY
Lying-in-State at Westminster to Begin Tomorrow. King Edward VIII Flies to the Privy Council. 'I am determined to follow in my father's footsteps.' King's Order for General Mourning. The body of King George will lie in state in Westminster Hall from tomorrow until Tuesday. The funeral will be on Tuesday at St George's Chapel, Windsor. There will be a State Procession from Westminster to Paddington Station.

Northern Echo, 22 January 1936

The proclamation of Edward VIII as king was read on 23 January 1936 by the Town Clerk, H. Hopkins, accompanied by the Mayor of Darlington, T.E. Hudson. The Abdication followed a short time later and it had a special significance for Darlington because the vicar of St Paul's Church, Revd R. Anderson Jardine, went to France to perform the wedding ceremony for the Duke and Duchess of Windsor.

DARLINGTON CEREMONY TODAY AT NOON

The Proclamation will be read from the steps of Darlington Town Hall at Noon today. The Education Committee had decided that the schools should be closed for the funeral of King George on Tuesday and that the schools should be closed at 11.30 a.m. instead of noon today so that children may hear the reading of the Proclamation. Before the business of this committee meeting, a vote of Consolation with the Queen and the Royal Family was passed. Ald Leach referred to the King as 'one who was honoured and loved as a father of the people'.

Northern Echo, 23 January 1936

QUEEN MARY WINS THE BLUE RIBAND; AND THE WHOLE COUNTRY CHEERS

Britain Holds The Blue Riband Again. The *Queen Mary*'s 30.63 knots, 2,929 miles Crossing In Under Four Days. Records Smashed on Consecutive Trips. Greeted by *Fox* off the Coast of Cornwall. The *Queen Mary* has won back for Britain the Blue Riband of the Atlantic, held for so long by the Tyne's *Mauretania*. She passed Bishop's Rock, Scilly Isles, at 8.12 last night (British Summer Time) having made the 2,929 mile crossing from Ambrose Light, off New York, in three days, 23 hours, 57 minutes. Her average speed was 30.63 knots, compared withg 30.31 knots which gained the Blue Riband for the French liner *Normandie* in June last year.

Northern Echo, 31 August 1936

Opposite: The man arrested after throwing a revolver at King Edward VIII is alleged to have said, 'The King was not hurt in any way, was he? I did not want to hurt him in any way. I only did it as a protest.' Here he is being led away.

THE KING: 'NO ATTEMPT AT ASSASSINATION'

Statement by Man Arrested after Revolver Throwing. Queen Mary, the Duke of Connaught and other members of the Royal Family, who had returned to the Palace by car, were entirely unaware of what had happened when they watched the King take the salute as the Guards marched past Buckingham Palace. It was not until members of the Royal family had gone into the Palace that they learned of the revolver incident. Queen Mary was one of the first to congratulate her son on his safe return.

Northern Echo, 17 July 1936

On the very day that Edward VIII abdicated, Harold W. Bettle, chief agent of the Durham group of the Conservative and Unionist Association, announced his resignation. Somehow, it did not have the same impact.

THE NEW KING EXPECTED TO TAKE THE TITLE OF GEORGE VI

King Edward to Broadcast Tonight 'as a Private Person' Mr Windsor. Farewell Message on leaving the country. His brother may confer a Dukedom on him. King Edward will broadcast a farewell message to the country tonight. . . . It is fixed tentatively for 10 p.m. After the King has spoken at 11 p.m. BBC transmitters will close down . . . The King's farewell to Parliament. 'After a long and anxious consideration I have determined to renounce the Throne to which I succeeded on the death of my father, and I am now communicating this, my final and irrevocable decision.'

Northern Echo, 11 December 1936

JARROW CRUSADE

Opposite top: [Prime Minister] Baldwin snubs Jarrow workers saying that it would be cowardice to receive the Jarrow marchers. 'This is the way in which civil strife begins and civil strife may not end until it is civil war.'

Women weep in the cheering crowds. 'You will maintain town's good name'. Mayor of Jarrow. The Jarrow march to London will take its place in the historic records of the borough and the remarkable scenes yesterday, when the 200 marchers left, will live long in the memory of those who took part and those who watched.

Northern Echo, 6 October 1936

Bottom: Jarrow marchers at a soup kitchen. They took a petition signed by people of all Tyneside asking for a revival of Jarrow's industries, which was to be presented to the government on 4 November.

Almost all the townspeople saw the start. Around the town Hall and along the route to Hebburn and then for some distance on the road to Chester-Le-Street where the men stayed last night, many thousands of people cheered. Again and again handkerchiefs waved and people shouted. 'God Speed' . . . When the roll was called, seven of the marchers failed to respond. One had got work and remained behind.

Northern Echo, 6 October 1936

> ### DARLINGTON CHOIR'S FINE SINGING. PHILHARMONIC SOCIETY'S ANNUAL CONCERT. FAMOUS SOPRANO
>
> Opportunities for hearing concerts of real merit in Darlington are so rare that the annual concert of the Darlington Philharmonic Society is always eagerly anticipated and it was not surprising to find the Co-operative Hall well filled on Wednesday evening. The Society arranged a programme which showed a commendable catholicity of taste. It included accompanied and unaccompanied songs and there were also four groups by Isobel Baillie, the well-know soprano.
>
> *Darlington & Stockton Times,*
> *18 February 1939*

Dame Isobel Baillie, the Scottish soprano, had very strong associations with Darlington. She had a magnificent voice and was the only British singer to appear three times with the conductor Toscanini. For many years she sang at Sir Henry Wood's Promenade Concerts in London.

'HAIL EDWARD'

The Duke and Duchess of Windsor in cordial greeting with Nazis. Flowers and cries of 'Hail Edward' greeted the Duke and Duchess of Windsor as they arrived in Berlin today.

The Duke and Herr Hitler Exchange Salutes. The Duke and Duchess of Windsor visited Herr Hitler in the German leader's mountain home near Berchtesgaden this afternoon and had tea with him. Herr Hitler bade farewell to his guests on the front steps of the chalet. He took the hand of the Duchess between both his hands and shook hands cordially. Then he turned to the Duke, shook hands with him and gave him the Nazi salute which the Duke returned.

Northern Echo, 23 October 1937

On 2 July 1938 Britain was bursting with pride when *Mallard*, king of steam engines, became the fastest locomotive in the world. With its designer, Nigel Gresley, on board to record its speed, it set an unassailable new world speed record for steam engines of 125 mph.

LNER Coronation Train's 125 Miles An Hour Record, Eleven Miles Faster Than Britain's Best. Held For 306 yards – Then Had To Shut Down for a Junction.

Northern Echo, 4 July 1938

'There's a
War On'

The first day of the war between Great Britain and Germany ended without any lightning blow from Germany. At all ARP posts there were reminders to carry gas masks, as this picture shows.

The King has appointed General Lord Gort Commander-in-Chief of the British Field Forces, General Sir Edmund Ironside Chief of the Imperial General Staff and General Sir Walter Kirk Commander-in-Chief of the Home Forces. The SS *Athenia* has been torpedoed in the Atlantic. Most of the passengers were women and children. German propaganda put out a ridiculous story that a British submarine, on Mr Churchill's orders, had sunk it to influence American opinion. At Middlesbrough yesterday, there were queues for gas masks. Yesterday while a congregation was praying that hostilities should be avoided even at the eleventh hour soldiers went swinging by to the music of 'Beer Barrel Polka'.

Northern Echo, 4 September 1939

Gas masks were issued to everyone, even babies, and, during the early months of the war, had to be carried all the time. Entrance to cinemas and other places of entertainment was banned unless you had your mask. As the war developed, these restrictions were relaxed. These children at an evacuation rehearsal are carrying gas masks.

GAS MASKS AT WEDDING
Miss Anne Bailey's bridegroom wore an ARP badge. Every guest carried a gas mask at the first war wedding at Bromptom Oratory yesterday. The bride, Miss Anne Bailey, second daughter of Sir Abe Bailey, the South African millionaire and sportsman, left her gas mask in the car. The bridegroom, Mr Pierce Synnott, took his to church but did not carry it to the altar. He wore an ARP badge in his button hole. Mr Synnott is one of the principals in the Secretary's Department of the Admiralty and was one of those who helped to arrange the 'Thetis' enquiry.

Northern Echo, 7 September 1939

Opposite: On 6 September it was announced at a special meeting of Redcar town council that an air-raid shelter was to be built under the promenade. Twenty more were to be bought, each to hold twenty people.

'Eat more carrots, then you'll be able to see in the dark', pundits advised. With the severe lighting restrictions now in force, carrots would be needed by the ton.

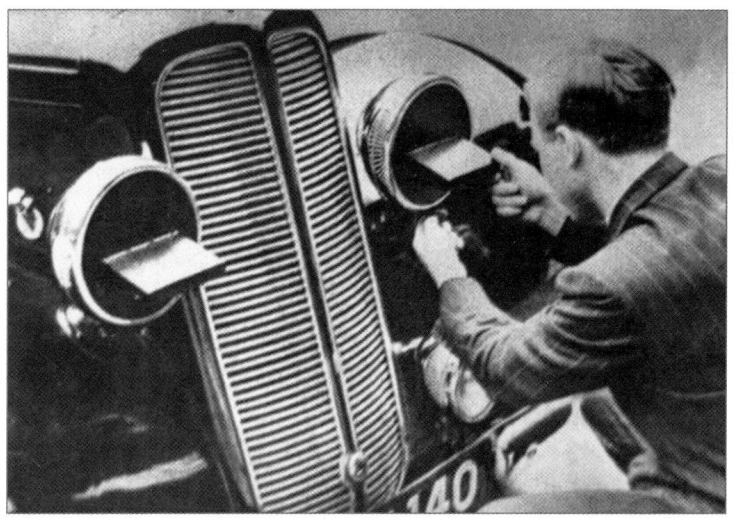

MORE CAR LIGHTING RESTRICTIONS

Direction Indicators Masked Down to ⅛ in Strip. Revised edition of the leaflet concerning the lighting for vehicles is available at police station. Points in addition to those stated by the Chief Constable of Durham given in the *Northern Echo* yesterday included: Rear lights: all openings other than the red rear light and stop light must be completely obscured. The red rear light must not exceed two inches in diameter and must be screened similarly to the red rear light. This means that there must be no longer any light illuminating the rear number plate. Direction indicators must be obscured except for a strip not exceeding an eighth of an inch in width. No other lights may be used except headlamps marked in the manner indicated in the leaflet.

Northern Echo, 7 September 1939

DARLINGTON TOWN COUNCIL: SHELTERS PROBLEM

Coun. Snowdon said he was concerned about shelter accommodation for those people who live in terrace houses where no Anderson Shelters [like the one pictured here] were available. He hoped they would give attention to this point in the more congested areas. Coun. Scott said that the question of the people living in areas where it was impossible to put up Anderson shelters was a matter of much concern to the Committee. So far the committee had received only 300 shelters. Another 300 were expected. The Corporation had already provided shelter for 3,000 people in trenches etc. They were now strengthening basements and making more shelters, but the difficulty was in getting the materials. Before many days were out they hoped to have shelter for 10,000 people.

Northern Echo, 8 September 1939

Patriotism embodied – young brothers Walter and Monty Buckley of Darlington in Army uniform. But if a six-year-old could drive a tractor, as the *Northern Echo* reported, they could learn to drive a tank.

BISHOP AUCKLAND BOY OF SIX DRIVES
HARVESTING TRACTOR

A boy of six, Alan Hicks, son of Mr John Hicks of Woodhouse Close Farm, Bishop Auckland, is making himself generally useful on his father's farm during the present harvest season. Each morning Alan rises early and takes his turn at cutting the corn with a tractor while his father superintends the efficient working of the self-binder. The boy drives the tractor unaided all around the field. Although very young, he has a mechanical mind. He stops and starts the engine like an experienced mechanic and has no difficulty in keeping a straight path with the tractor.

Northern Echo, 8 September 1939

The one thing unaffected by the war was the British sense of humour, as this blackout cartoon illustrates.

"I've been trying to make up my mind whether she's showing too much light."

Opposite: Blackout precautions were only a few of many necessary wartime inconveniences to which people quickly became adjusted. Strips of adhesive paper fixed to windows to reduce the risk of flying glass, as shown here, became commonplace; and it was not unusual for 'the best laid schemes o' mice an' men' to 'gang aft a – gley', as this *Northern Echo* report shows.

AIR RAID BUZZER THREE MILES AWAY. SEDGEFIELD PARISH COUNCILLORS CONCERNED

The official intimation of an air raid at Sedgefield will be the blowing of a buzzer at Fishburn, three miles away. At yesterday's meeting of Sedgefield Parish Council, Coun. R. McMillan was of the opinion that the buzzer would be inaudible at Sedgefield when the wind was blowing in the wrong direction. He had consulted the Area ARP Officer with a view to the siren being sounded at the Durham County Hospital of Winterton, but was given to understand that the hospital was not included on the official list to receive a warning. Coun. McMillan said it was the duty of the Council to see that Sedgefield was protected and he thought representation should be made to the Chief Constable to get the hospital included on the receiving list. This was agreed to.

Northern Echo, 15 September 1939

This painting by artist Phil May depicts Flying Officer G.M. Bennions of No. 41 Squadron in a Spitfire shooting down a Messerschmitt over Teesdale. The German plane crashed near Barnard Castle.

THE REAL AIR WAR BEGINS

The real air was is beginning at last. That is the opinion in aeronautical circles here. This week has already seen more activity in the air from the Shetlands to the lower extremities of the Franco–German frontier than in any other corresponding periods since the outbreak of war. New types of aircraft have gradually been introduced into service by the German High Command during the last week or two and, more significant still, larger formations of aircraft are now being utilised.

Northern Echo, 4 April 1940

Opposite: The women pictured here all worked in the Army laundry at School Aycliffe during the war. They and other women regularly organised events in support of local 'Comforts for the Troops' appeals.

WHEATLEY HILL UNITED WOMEN'S WAR COMMITTEE

At a meeting of Wheatley Hill United Women's War Committee it was announced that Sherburn Hill Co-operative Society, as the result of a local effort, had given £8 12s to the Wheatley Hill Comforts Fund. Miss Gowland had raised £2 more. The Council School Teachers contributed monthly and members of the British Legion 'did their bit'. The Wesleyans had offered to give a concert and another effort to help funds. A total of £183 had been raised to provide Comforts and Easter Gifts.

Northern Echo, 3 May 1940

Wartime vogues, like the outfit modelled here, were divorced from the reality experienced by most people.

GET MORE WEAR OUT OF YOUR CLOTHES

'Darn for Victory'. Clothes will have to be made to last longer. A New Board of Trade order restricting wholesalers' sales of cotton, rayon, and linen to 75 per cent of pre-war quantities is not expected to produce shortage this summer for shops have laid big stocks, but if any future shortage is to be avoided, the public will have to get more wear out of their clothes. In other words, they must mend instead of spend and the slogan 'Darn for Victory' may yet become as well known as 'Dig for Victory'. Affected by the restrictions are almost everything a woman wears, men's shirts to a lesser degree and such articles of domestic utility as table cloths, pillow cases and handkerchiefs.

Northern Echo, 17 April 1940

Percy Robson, Secretary of the Hartlepool branch of the Dunkirk Veterans Association, showing justifiable pride in the part he and the Durham Light Infantry played in the evacuation of the British Expeditionary Force from Dunkirk.

DUNKIRK EVACUATION

The withdrawal has been carried out in the face of intense and almost continuous air attack and increasing artillery and machine gun fire. It was undertaken on the British side by several flotillas of destroyers and a large number of small craft of every description. This force was rapidly increased and a total of 222 British naval vessels and 665 other British craft and boats took part in the operation. These figures do not include large numbers of French Naval and merchant ships which also played their part.

Northern Echo, 4 June 1940

Opposite: The Home Guard, ATC, Civil Defence Cadet Corps (the Darlington Branch is pictured here) and other Civil Defence organisations quickly sprang up – and very good they were too! This letter in praise of the Home Guard could apply equally well to any of the other Civil Defence groups.

PRAISE FOR THE HOME GUARD

It has done my heart good to see a new corps of the Home Guard at our work jump to it in the grandest spirit as in all other part of the town and country. The highest praise is due to the Army officers and the NCOs as well as ex-servicemen instructors who use the best means of getting the men into their stride. Among these men are the makings of fine soldiers. They may be able to do valuable work in relieving 'regulars' if the need should arise. They will be among England's best defenders. Yours etc. Ex-soldier Darling, 6 September.

Northern Echo, 7 September 1940

Farming like coal mining has been designated a reserved occupation, so farmers are not called up for National Service. Cattle dealers, who are not food producers, who call themselves farmers, are also excused call up to the armed forces by a Government that should know better.

RESERVED AGE LOWERED TO 18 IN MAIN GROUPS

In view of the importance of increased home food production, the Government, the Ministry of Agriculture announced last night, has decided to lower the age of reservation from 21 to 18 in four of the more important groups in the agricultural industry.

Northern Echo, 7 June 1940

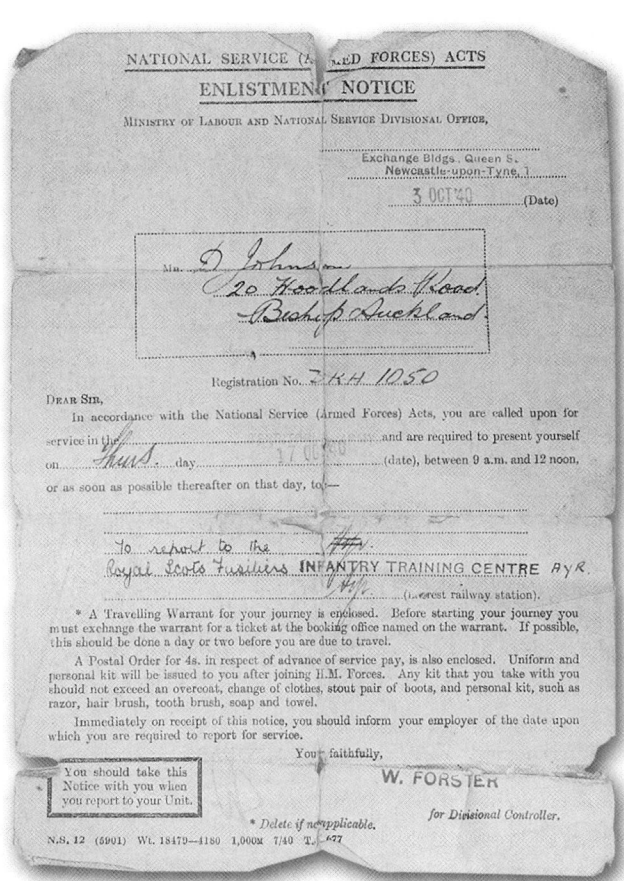

Unless they were in a reserved occupation, people received their call up papers within days of their eighteenth birthday. The enlistment notice was straight to the point – 'you are called upon for service . . .' – ignore it at your peril. By this means, losses in manpower were made good and the numerical requirements of the Armed forces were fulfilled.

> **LOSSES IN AIR FIGHTING**
> **OVER BRITAIN**
> Following are figures of German planes destroyed and British planes and pilots lost since mass raids on this country started on 11 August: 2,137 German planes brought down between 11 August and 2 October: 1,879 by RAF: 256 by AA: 2 by Balloon barrage. British machines lost, 601: pilots lost 283.
>
> *Northern Echo*, 3 October 1940

These workers at a munitions factory near Heighington look reasonably content with their lot; but is this brave face just for the camera? At one 'war factory', unspecified because of wartime restrictions, all was not well.

CONDITIONS AT A DURHAM FACTORY

Sir, Several correspondents have complained of conditions at a war factory in Co. Durham. Hundreds of the girls have to rise before 4 a.m. with between one and two miles to walk to catch a train at 5 a.m., and this to start the morning shift at 6.45 a.m.! Many of them do not get home until after 5 at night. They are away from home 13 hours for an 8½ hour shift. Sometimes the internal transport system fails and leaves the girls waiting half an hour, sometimes in the rain. The food at the canteen is not always all it might be and the prices are not low. Do these things inspire the best work? – that is what Britain needs. Yours etc. One of them.

Northern Echo, 12 November 1941

Opposite: The swastika is a primitive religious symbol in the shape of a cross, usually with the ends of the arms bent at right angles, either in a clockwise or an anti-clockwise direction. In 1935 this representation, with arms bent clockwise, was officially adopted as the emblem of Nazi Germany. To the Allies it and all it stood for became despised.

WE'LL BEAT HITLER

One of Middlesbrough's most active nonagenarians, appropriately named Mrs Mary Ann Old, was celebrating her ninetieth birthday with her married daughter, Mrs Thompson, with whom she lives, and her seventy-two-year-old sister. 'We'll beat Hitler', she told me [a *Northern Echo* reporter] confidentially when I asked her about the war. 'I never thought I'd see such a "carry on" as this'. A native of Cockerton, Mrs Old has lived in Middlesbrough for over seventy-five years.

Northern Echo, 9 October 1940

On the evening of 19 November 1941 British advance forces captured Sidi Rezegh, South East of Tobruk, and on the following day battle was joined with strong German Command Forces. After losing seventy tanks, thirty-three armoured cars and several hundred prisoners, the Germans withdrew. The casualties were not all on the German side, as this picture of British Tanks at Sidi Rezegh shows. Throughout the campaign in the Western desert the Durham Light Infantry was part of what became the celebrated Desert Rats. While pressure was rapidly exerted on the Axis forces holding defensive positions from Halfaya to Sidi Omar, British armoured foundations, supported by New Zealand, South African and Indian troops crossed the frontier south of Sidi Oman.

William Henry Bennison of Hartlepool, an experienced coxwain, joined the Royal Navy where he qualified as a lieutenant. He went on to distinguish himself, as his medals testify. His was an excellent 'call up' experience. Others left much to be desired.

DARLINGTON WOMAN OF 73 CALLED UP FOR WAR WORK

Sir, on 1 April my mother, who is seventy-three, got her calling up papers for National Service. She was ill at the time. Remembering the date, she took it as a good joke. But it was carried further. Last week the policeman called because she had not answered the call. After seeing her identity card and pension book the policeman said that he would put it right for her. But the joke is going too far now. She got her papers again this week, demanding that she should go and take her identity card and birth certificate with her. Who is responsible for these blunders? Yours etc. Annoyed.

Northern Echo, 4 May 1942

Opposite: The town of Bardia, which had been occupied by the New Zealanders on 22 November and recaptured by the enemy on 1 December, surrendered unconditionally to British and Imperial forces on 2 January after a brilliant attack in which Polish and Free French forces took part. Pictured are Germans captured in a Durham Light Infantry attack.

ROMMEL IN FLIGHT AGAIN

Withdrawal From Agedabia Under Cover of Sandstorm. Rommel is once more in retreat in the Western Desert. The Middle East War communiqué issued from British GHQ yesterday states: Taking advantage of a heavy sandstorm, which continues severely to restrict visibility, the enemy is withdrawing from Agedabia, covered by strong rearguards. Our mobile columns of all arms are moving forward in pursuit over a wide front. Progress, however, has been slow owing particularly to weather conditions and also to the use made by the enemy of extensive mine fields.

Northern Echo, 9 January 1942

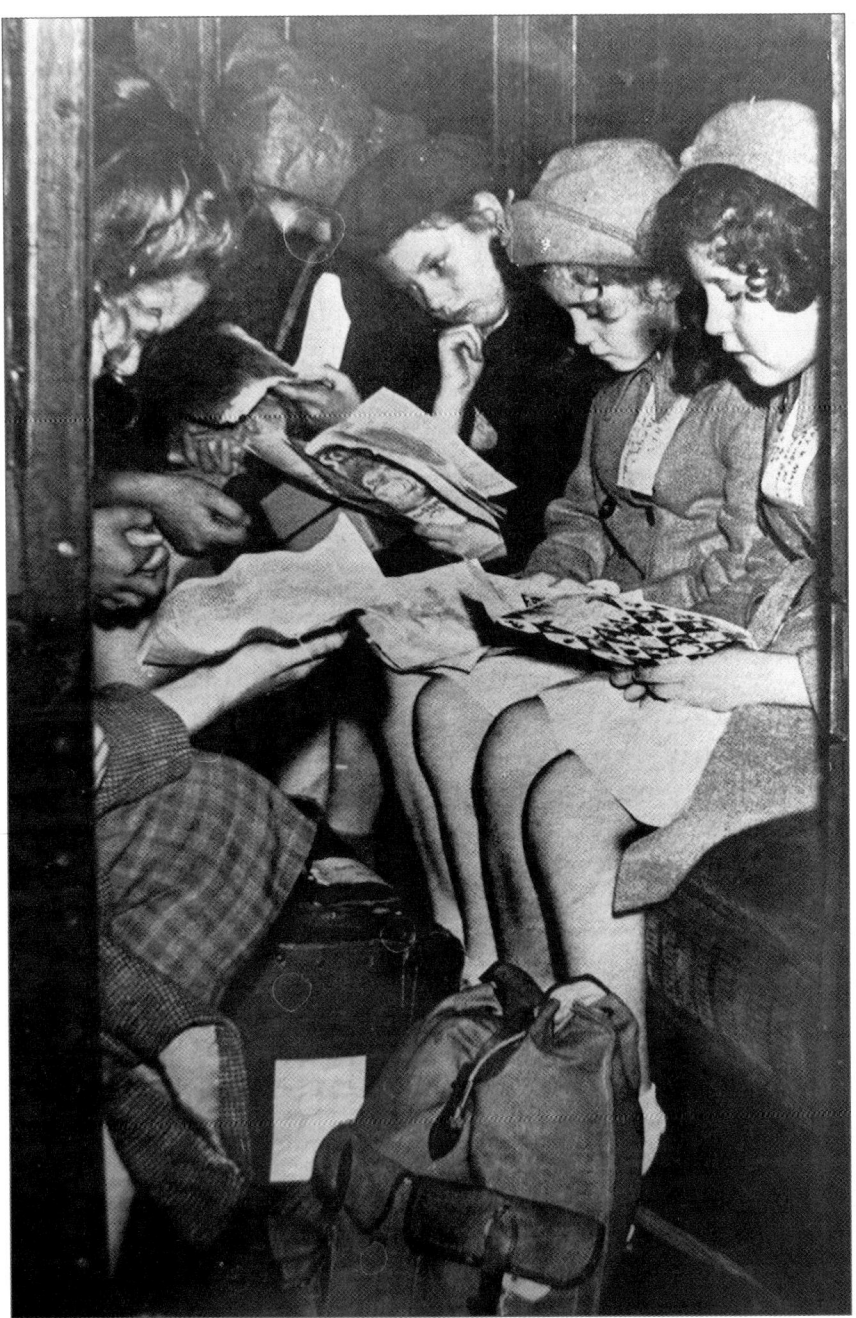

In 1944 Germany's new secret weapon was a long-range shell with a trajectory akin to that of an ordinary shell but assisted by an auxiliary engine. Many London children, some of whom are pictured here in the North-East, were evacuated from the capital because of this new threat to their lives.

PILOTLESS PLANES ARE UNDER 20 FEET LONG. LONG-RANGE SHELL WITH AUXILIARY ENGINE
Some details of the German's much-vaunted secret weapon, the pilotless plane, were released last night. Observers say that those midget planes, like a Spitfire in shape only much smaller, are painted a dark brown or black. They fly at high speed but low altitude, keeping on a straight course, and emit a distinctive rhythmic note similar to a two stroke.

Northern Echo, 17 June 1944

NO PENSION FOR BLACKHALL MOTHER OF BOY SAILOR
Sir, may I thank Sailor's Mother for the praise she has given to a plucky little fellow? My own son joined the Merchant Navy and went to North Russia at the age of 16, but, alas, did not return. I was told by a survivor that my son had always done a man's work, and I shall always be proud that he did his duty. On the other hand we mothers do expect a little recompense. Although I have eight children under 10½, I could not get either compensation or pension. I was told my son had not been in the Seamen's Union long enough. Yours etc. Catherine Hoole, Middle Street, Blackhall, Co. Durham 5 April.

Northern Echo, 7 April 1943

Pilot Officer William McMullen, a French Canadian, was returning to his base at Middleton St George when the Lancaster he was piloting developed serious engine problems. He stayed at the controls of his plane until his crew had parachuted to safety and he was clear of Darlington town centre.

GUIDED HIS CRASHING PLANE AWAY FROM TOWN.
PILOT KILLED NEAR DARLINGTON

The pilot of a plane is thought to have lost his life in successfully preventing his plane from crashing on Darlington on Saturday night. All other members of the crew are reported to have bailed out successfully before the plane crashed. They are stated to have left the plane thinking that the pilot would follow them. Many people in Darlington heard the plane over the town and from the noise of the engines felt that it was in difficulties. A few saw the navigation lights as it circled over the town and hearing the unusual noise feared that it would crash. 'It seemed to circle round', said one man, 'and looked as though it was going to drop somewhere in the town. Then it turned away east and a few seconds later we heard a crash followed by a few muffled explosions and the glare of a fire.' It crashed on Lingfield Farm on the Darlington to Middleton St George road owned by Mr G. Thompson. It hit a Dutch barn in which was stored a large quantity of vats and barley.

Northern Echo, 13 January 1945

It was a time for celebration and remembrance, a time for pride and magnanimity. It was a brief respite, for the war against Japan continued unabated.

TODAY IS V-DAY-OFFICIAL

Germans Sign Surrender To Three Allied Powers. Victory has come not alone through the planning of the captains and the statesmen, but by the resolution of the common people – the warden at the CD post, the worker in the factory and on the land, the housewife in the queue. In this cavalcade their place is symbolised by Churchill, Roosevelt and Stalin. The Admirals, the Generals and the Air Marshalls can appear only in selection. Nor when we think of Dowding and the Battle of Britain, of Montgomery and the Rhine, must we forget such men as Mitchell of the Spitfires and Bailey of the bridges.

Northern Echo, 8 May 1945

FORGOTTEN ARMY

Sir, may I compliment your London correspondent on what he says about the lack of news . . . given to the deeds of the largest single British Army fighting the toughest foe on the world's worst battle front – the forgotten army. Hundreds of thousands of relatives of these boys are waiting to hear about their deeds but the powers that be are silent. Why? I am the father of one of the 7th Indian Division – out there. Yours etc. R. Jackson, 57 Brunswick Street, Stockton. 14 June.

Northern Echo, 18 June 1945

'There's a Peace On'

During the war, the usual response to requests for anything in short supply or unobtainable was 'Don't you know, there's a war on?' During the early postwar years the usual response was 'Don't you know, there's a peace on?' for the same reason. These tanks rolling along Northgate, Darlington, were part of the town's victory celebrations. Austerity could not dampen the spirits.

HOW THE NORTH-EAST CELEBRATED VICTORY

Darlington Crowded: Middlesbrough Quiet. Victory Day was celebrated in the North-East on Saturday with parades, children's sports and teas, fireworks and bonfires, and, in several cases, thanksgiving services were held.

Crowds began to assemble on High Row, Darlington, several hours before the Victory procession came along and when the Mayor (Coun. Ben Dodd) took his place at the saluting base the centre of the town was packed with thousands of enthusiastic spectators. The Mayor was accompanied by members of the Town Council and Colonel A.N. Venning represented the GOC Northumbrian Division.

Northern Echo, 10 June 1946

Heavy falls of drifting snow in the 'hap-up' of 1947 brought the country to its knees. Isolated hill farmers suffered severe losses among their sheep. Provisions and fodder were dropped by helicopter – the only way to deliver them because so many roads were blocked. The railway line between Darlington and Kirkby Stephen was closed for nine weeks.

TWELVE HOUR ELECTRICITY CUT THREATENED

Worst winter since 1940. Most roads snow and ice bound. The longest cut in the electricity current so far – from 7 a.m. to 7 p.m. – may be made today. Announcing this, Central Electricity Board once more emphasised that there may be no option unless people voluntarily reduce consumption. The warning came after a day of the most severe cuts experienced yet, leading to blackouts over wide districts, interruption of work in factories and interference with transport.

Northern Echo, 30 January 1947

DARLINGTON MAN'S CLIMB UP HIGH FORCE

Few visitors to High Force in Teesdale are likely to have seen that beauty spot from the same angle as Mr Walter Bainbridge of Westlands Road, Darlington, a member of the Pease and Partners estate office staff. Earlier this year while at Middleton-in-Teesdale, a friend, Mr Vincent Rodgers . . . thought the rock face of High Force would offer an interesting challenge and propounded a plan to traverse the buttress of the rock from the Durham side to the waterfall on the Yorkshire side and then climb the frontal portion. With Mr Rodgers and his brother, Mr Bainbridge set off for the ascent one Saturday and roped up at about 9.30 a.m. on the Durham side over which no water was falling. . . . [Mr Bainbridge] had to obtain a three-finder hold with the left hand and then stretch out his leg to the ledge, preserving his balance by inserting the tips of his right hand into a thin track. 'Below, at each of [the] ticklish places was a drop of some 50 feet,' said Mr Bainbridge, 'and I was painfully aware of the precariousness of my position.'

Darlington & Stockton Times, 14 December 1946

This photograph shows High Force, the formidable target of climbers Walter Bainbridge and Vincent and Tom Rodgers in 1946.

One-time BBC news reader Wilfred Pickles famously lost that job because, in the days of correct articulation, he closed his bulletins with a broad Yorkshire, 'good neet'. His eight-week tour of mining areas with his radio programme *Have A Go* included mines in the Durham coalfield.

WILFRED AND MABEL WILL TALK TO MINERS

Wilfred Pickles and his wife, Mabel, will take the 'Have A Go' programme on an eight-week tour of mining areas as part of a scheme to focus national attention on the fuel crisis. The itinerary will extend from Scotland to South Wales with the first programme at Doncaster towards the end of the month. Some of the programmes may be bradcast. The final arrangements for the scheme were settled in London yesterday at an hour's conference between Mr and Mrs Pickles, divisional representatives of the Coal Board and Ministry of Fuel and Power officials. Afterwards, Mr Pickles said, 'The miner is on the front line of the National effort today and deserves your full support'.

Northern Echo, 6 February 1951

Seen here on 20 July 1955 in the grounds of The Palace of Nations, Geneva, a relaxed Sir Anthony Eden is seated with other heads of government at a four-powers conference: left to right, Marshall Bulganin (Russia), President Eisenhower (USA), and Edgar Faure (France). On 16 April the preceding year, Mr Eden was preparing for an election, which he won.

SIR ANTHONY EDEN TELLS NATION 26 MAY IS THE DAY! PARTIES SWING INTO ACTION.

The question of a general election has now been decided. In a two minute broadcast on radio and television last night, the Prime Minister, Sir Anthony Eden, announced that the dates would be: Dissolution, Friday 6 May; Polling Day, Thursday 26 May; Newly Elected Parliament Meets, 7 June; State Opening, 14 June. Sir Anthony said in his broadcast, 'The announcement I want to make to you tonight is an important one and I thought I should give it to you myself. The Parliament elected in 1951 is now in its fourth year. It is therefore not surprising that with a change of Prime Minister, there should be expectation of a general election.'

Northern Echo, 26 April 1954

THE STATE OF THE PARTIES IN THE 1954 GENERAL ELECTION

The gains and losses in the following are based on divisions which have not undergone boundary changes. 'Conservative' includes Conservative and supporters.

Conservatives 343 seats – 11 gains – 1 loss
Labour 277 seats – 1 gain – 10 losses
Liberal 5 seats – nil – nil
Others 2 seats – 2 gains – 3 losses

Northern Echo, 29 May 1954

Winter weather is no respector of human activities, be they work or play, as this inspection of a snowbound Darlington FC pitch illustrates. 'Follow the Quakers', the sign exhorts. Where to? The nearest pub by the look of the pitch.

SAGGING UNDER WEIGHT OF SNOW

Snow, ice, slush fog and floods were the ingredients of a New Year's Day weather mixture, which delayed traffic on many roads in the North and in Scotland and brought many accidents. Yorkshire was the worst hit English county, according to a Royal Automobile Club spokesman. The Leeds telephone manager said that over 2,000 telephones were out of order because of wires which fell or sagged under the weight of snow. The RAC reported last night that conditions were worsening.

SNOW TAKEN BY LORRY TO SKI SLOPE, GARMISCH, BAVARIA

Snow has had to be brought from as far as 25 miles during the past three days to the Olympic Ski jump here so that the second stage of the New Year ski jump competition could be carried out.

Northern Echo, 2 January 1958

People are football mad in the North-East but they do indulge in other activities. It is surprising what took place behind the façade of North Road workshops, seen here.

> ### DARLINGTON TEAM AT YORK TO RAILWAY FIRE-FIGHTING FINALS
> The North Road Locomotive Works, Darlington, won their way through to the finals of the British Railway fire-fighting competitions when they won the five-man trailer pump drill in the North-Eastern finals at York yesterday. In spite of incurring a penalty of three seconds, they completed the exercise in one minute, eight seconds better than the runners up, York Carriage and Water Works.
> *Northern Echo*, 11 May 1955

Skinnergate, Darlington, looking away from its junction with Coniscliffe Road, the subject of a reader's letter to the *Northern Echo*.

DRIVING ON THE RIGHT AT A DARLINGTON ROAD JUNCTION

Sir, may I, through 'Hear All Sides', address a direct question or two to Durham County Police? Is it lawful to drive on the wrong side of the road (and consequently the wrong side of the opposing traffic stream) at the turning from Skinnergate to Coniscliffe Road, Darlington? Would the driver of a police car be expected to wait (if necessary through several light changes) for a chance to cross on the correct side whenever traffic conditions would allow, or would he be in order to cross on the wrong side? The sight, the other day, of a young girl cyclist who, obeying the lights, wobbled forward between a heavy lorry going northwards (as she was herself) and a car turning from Skinnergate to Coniscliffe Road on the wrong side had promoted these questions. There are very few inches to spare on either side of this cyclist and it seemed wrong that any set of lights would invite cyclists to ride between two lines of motor vehicles. A clear answer from the police to these questions would be most helpful.

If it is unlawful to drive on the wrong side at this corner the practice should be stopped. If it is perfectly lawful there should be indications on the roadway telling the driver what he is expected to do. Yours etc. witness.

[A senior police officer told the *Northern Echo* yesterday, that it is not unlawful to drive on the right at the turning from Skinnergate to Coniscliffe Road. Drivers must use common sense and judgement and not drive in the face of oncoming traffic.]

Northern Echo, 23 August 1958

There was a bad start to the 1960/1 season for Darlington Football Club and it had nothing to do with how the team played.

It was smoking as usual on trolleys like the one pictured here, but the wind of change was blowing through the top of Darlington's double-deckers.

STOP SMOKING ON BUSES BY REQUEST

Smokers puffing away on the top deck of Darlington Corporation buses may soon be politely requested to put them out. The town's Transport Committee proposes that notices to this effect be displayed on the upper deck and in the rear saloon of single-deckers. The suggestion comes before Thursday's Council meeting. 'There will be no enforcement', said the chairman of the committee, Ald. L.G. Turner, 'just notices requesting passengers not to smoke.' He thought conductors were too busy to make sure the request was obeyed.

Northern Echo, 28 September 1964

NORTH-EAST TRIES HARD WITH SOFT TOUCH

For an outlay of £200 tonight the North-East Development Council expects to bring thousands of pounds worth of industrial development into the region. The £200 is the cost of booking a conference room as Claridges, the London hotel for two and a half hours of hard-sell discussions with 50 southern industrialists.'

Northern Echo, 9 November 1967

Coronation Street's Elsie Tanner (actress Pat Phoenix) is pictured here at the Tyne Bridge, Newcastle, and in 1967 she was very much in the news.

WHERE WAS ELSIE WHEN THE LIGHT WENT OUT?

Mrs Elizabeth Sinclair feared for *Coronation Street*'s Elsie Tanner – until I [reporter Frank Johnson] told her yesterday that she'd turned up in the 'Rover's Return'. Mrs Sinclair, who lives in a farm cottage between South Hetton and Haswell, was completely in the dark about the TV serial's 'train disaster' last week because of two power cuts. 'I am not a great follower of the series', said Mrs Sinclair in her cottage at Fallowfield Farm. 'But after so much advance publicity about someone being written out of *Coronation Street* I decided not to miss last week's episode. On Monday the electricity was off from lunch time until 9.30 p.m. I thought I could 'catch up' by watching on Wednesday, but the electricity went off again for 3½ hours from 5 p.m. so I missed both nights and it was a tremendous disappointment.'

Northern Echo, 16 May 1967

IF YOU GO DOWN TO THE WOODS TODAY

Usually it's we humans who get the surprise when we venture down to the woods, but from now on the surprise is on the teddy bears. For when they toddle into Deepdale [pictured here] with their picnic hampers this week they will find all the paths clear with steps cut into the steep banks down to the picturesque river. For some years the bears, together with human ramblers, were forbidden to go into the area because the Army used it as a shooting range.

When the Army moved out six years ago the once popular paths through the woods became overgrown and blocked by fallen trees. And so they stayed – until Saturday. Then, armed with saws, axes, and spades, the volunteers moved in, some from the Teesdale Civic Society, some from the inter-denominational Barnard Castle youth club and some just keen ramblers. Their aim was to clear the paths to the Cat Castle railway; and they set to work in a steady drizzle . . . There were thirty people in the woods – it was the first time in Deepdale for seventeen-year-old Howard Stainthorpe, a local boy. 'Up to now I didn't know it existed', he said, 'but I'll certainly come back now the paths are clear'. Let's hope the teddy bears do too.

Northern Echo, 13 November 1967

In 1971 traditional rivals Wearside and Tyneside joined forces to become part of a new metropolitan county.

SUPER COUNTIES WILL WIPE OUT 70 COUNCILS

A Government axe is poised to wipe out more than half the North-East's local councils. In a white paper on the re-organisation of local government, the North-East's 120 councils will be cut down to about 50. The White Paper, which is the Tories' answer to the Maud Report, was published yesterday and is intended to come into force on 1 April 1974. It plans a major shake up of local government, replacing 1,210 local councils in England by 54 new county authorities and 334 subordinate district councils. Under the new proposals, County Durham will lose all its coastline to two new counties centred on Newcastle and Teeside. It will, however, gain a small slice of the North Riding, comprising the Croft and Startforth local authority areas. Northumberland will lose its south-east corner to the Newcastle-based county.

Northern Echo, 17 February 1971

Mary and Joseph (Emma Jeffrey, on the donkey, and Andrew Taylor) are doing a dress rehearsal for the nativity play at Brompton-on-Swale school in 1989. In 1971 a North-Riding vicar gave the festive period a novel twist. He planned to prevent anyone with more than his or her share of Christmas spirit from attending Christmas Midnight Mass. This was received with decidedly saturnalian response.

NO ROOM AT THE INN

Vicar's 'Avoid The Drunks' Scheme Angers Town. A North Riding vicar's plan to stop drunks coming to Christmas Midnight Mass – by moving the service out of town to a village without a pub – has started a rumpus. Regular drinkers in Helmsley's five pubs are seething at the move by the town's vicar, the Revd David Senior, who plans to hold the service in Pockley, a dry village.

   Mr Bernard Peterson, aged 25, took a swallow from his pint in the Black Swan Hotel last night and said, 'Most people I have talked to think the vicar has got a bit of a cheek. Just because you have a drink on Christmas Eve it does not mean you can't go to Midnight Mass. I certainly won't be driving to Pockley – it the police get to know about this, they will be waiting along the road to breathalyse people. The vicar has spoilt the start of Christmas for a lot of people in Helmsley.'

Northern Echo, 16 December 1971

During severe winter weather like that in 1973 table scraps may make all the difference to birds, like the blackbird pictured here on its springtime nest with young.

DON'T FORGET TO FEED THE BIRDS

The recent heavy snowfall, hard frosts and biting winds seem to indicate we are in for a hard winter as the weather prophets predicted. To ensure that food scraps don't find their way into the kitchen wastebin, my wife [Mrs Ray Kennedy] keeps a small plastic dish near the sink unit and all the leftovers are emptied straight into this, providing the birds with a variety of titbits. Water is also of great importance to our birds, not only for drinking but for bathing, because even in the coldest weather many birds enjoy a bath. An inverted dustbin lid or something similar set into the ground makes an ideal bath as the varying depth allows even the tiny blue-tit to complete daily toilet. A few drops of glycerine will prevent the water from freezing over.

Northern Echo, 20 December 1973

Desperate situations demand desperate measures. In 1973 the British Steel Corporation announced big cutbacks in steel production throughout the North-East, the Tyne lost three ship repair contracts and two more went to Swan Hunter at North Shields.

BRITISH STEEL ORDERS MASSIVE CUTBACK IN PRODUCTION

A big cutback in steel production throughout the North-East was announced by the British Steel Corporation yesterday. A spokesman for the Teesside and Workington Group of the General Steels Division said that over the Christmas holiday period, when no coal would be delivered to the steelworks, production would drop to about 40 per cent of the normal levels . . . From the New Year, however, the steel corporation said it hoped to continue steel making close to current output levels, but this depended on coal supplies being resumed at current levels – about 30 per cent below normal deliveries because of the miners' overtime ban.

Northern Echo, 20 December 1973

The Old Order Changeth

When Peter Tod became director of Darlington's Civic Theatre it marked a change of fortune for the town's beautiful Edwardian playhouse. Under his inspired direction it quickly became acknowledged as the brightest jewel in Darlington's crown and recognised throughout the theatrical profession as one of the most important provincial theatres in the country. Peter Tod is pictured here with a 'House Full' notice.

IT'S TIME FOR PANTOMIME
Peter Tod, director of Darlington's Civic Theatre, said recently that for theatre people, Christmas meant pantomime. . . . Darlington plumps for a very traditional pantomime, *Sleeping Beauty*, done in traditional manner – though the principal boy is actually a boy. Tom Mennard plays Queen Everbrite.

Northern Echo, 22 December 1973

Cricket takes its place alongside football in North-East's sporting heart and Darlington teams have long featured prominently in the news. This is Darlington Seconds in 1976. Back row, left to right: J. Vart, R. Jackson, C. Bowes, A. Thompson, A. Johnson, J.E. Edwardson; front row: J. MacMillan, T. Dobson, C. Camburn, C. Harrison, J. Reynolds.

Opposite: Crime used to be associated to some degree with poor housing conditions like the gas-lit Victorian terrace, seen here in an advanced state of decay. In an increasingly affluent society, instead of falling, as one would expect, crime and violence continue to climb.

HELLS ANGELS DENY BEATING UP PERFECT STRANGER

Three Hells Angels attacked and beat up a perfect stranger in a town centre, a court was told yesterday. '[A labourer] was punched to the ground and kicked a number of times by all three', said Mr Oliver Wrightson, prosecuting at Durham Crown Court.

[The three men denied] assaulting Mr Wallace, occasioning him actual bodily harm.

Mr Wrightson said that [the victim] had just said goodnight to a friend in Darlington and was on his way to catch the last bus home when he was attacked. 'The three men approached [the victim]', he said, 'and [one], after saying something to him, punched [the victim] in the face without any warning. The other two then joined in and knocked [the victim] to the ground where he was kicked about the head a number of times'.

The three men were arrested later the same evening after police found them in a fish shop. They denied throughout that they were involved in the attack. However, blood was found on [one's] boots and [another's] jeans.

Northern Echo, 2 October 1974

The Post Office increased the cost of posting Christmas cards and was greeted by a storm of protest.

BLOW TO TRADITION

Reports suggesting the death of the Christmas card may prove to be exaggerated. But, thanks to the cost of postage, sales are 30 per cent down. Shops are full of half price cards and an enterprising York business is going to the root of the trouble by selling stamps with 1½ off. The card trade has certainly been set back a few years, for more than most it depends on continuity; when second cousin Mildred strikes you off, she will not lightly restore you.

Does it please the Post Office, which at least has saved the wages of many seasonal part-timers? Almost certainly not and, while there is still a rush for fewer people, it cannot be the same in post offices – where the Christmas rush has been a morale-booster, with a sort of wartime camaraderie – to know that everyone with relatives and friends within walking distance is his or her own postman this year. It is nice to feel wanted. The Hear All Sides correspondent who told of buying 15 stamps instead of her usual 48 may be a more determined walker than most, but her stand is not untypical. The Post Office argues that sheer economics have forced price increases, which run the risk of being self-defeating. Surely, though, greetings cards are a special case, and not just for sentimental reasons; of course there will be consumer resistance when the postage can be three times the cost of the card itself. Next year the Post Office should look again at the idea of selling, perhaps in the summer, lower-price stamps for use on unsealed envelopes during the middle fortnight of December. The early takings would be money in the bank, and last-minute chaos at counters and in sorting offices would be eased. And if the Post Office was feeling really imaginative it could even explore the idea, apparently being pioneered by freelancers, of interesting garages in giving postage stamps as an alternative to Green Shield stamps.

Northern Echo, 18 December 1975

On Saturday 3 January 1976 severe gales and floods played havoc with northern football fixtures – and that was just for starters. Trees collapsed wholesale, as shown here.

GALES RIP THE NORTH TO SHREDS

The North-East reeled under severe gales and floods last night as it received its heaviest battering for many years. City and town centres were in chaos with trees blown over, shop fronts blown out and power cuts throughout the region. In Weardale five old people were trapped when the gable end of an old people's home collapsed at Stanhope. Two of them were rescued by the fire brigade and the other three managed to get out by themselves, it is understood. Ambulance, the fire brigade and social service officials were standing by at the home, Weardale House, early today, prepared to evacuate the rest of the residents, as the house was said to be in a dangerous condition.

Local newsagent, Mr Ian Rowland, said: 'It's like a battlefield from one end of the dale to the other. I've never seen anything like it in my life. There are floods, gales, blackout and now this roof collapse. The firemen are doing everything they can to get them out.'

Newcastle Weather Centre reported gale force nine over much of the North-East with storm force ten gusts in places. Off the north-east coast, gusts of wind reached over 100 mph.

Northern Echo, 3 January 1976

When Darlington's National School, pictured here, was built, for pupils to be caned by the head for disruptive behaviour was a normal, accepted and highly effective method of maintaining school discipline. It was a school matter and kept within those confines. In 1976 before such punishment could be meted out the pupil's parents had to be consulted and the culprit was asked whether he or she had any objection. Times change but change is not always progress.

TYNESIDE HEAD CANES TWO GIRLS

Just four days after the 'gymslip riot' in Newcastle, a Tyneside headmaster has caned two 15-year-old girls who blacked another girl's eye because she did not invite them to the Christmas party.

Mr Donald Simpson, head of Linskill High School, North Shields, said yesterday: 'They accepted their punishment without raising any objections and they have apologised for what they did. The girl they hit suffered pain and I think there was only one way of dealing with them.'

He said he had the backing of the punished girls' parents. 'The offensive thing is that the girls stored up a grudge and attacked this girl when they returned to school last week after the Christmas holidays', said Mr Simpson. 'The school council, which has representatives of every form, fully supports any action I take to stamp out violence.'

Northern Echo, 13 January 1976

'How do you spell it?' D-A-R-L-I-N-G-T-O-N
'Who are the greatest?' D-A-R-L-I-N-G-T-O-N
'Who's going to Wembley?' D-A-R-L-I-N-G-T-O-N

Not this year: maybe next! Quakers fans, 1977.

MOURNERS HAVE TO WALK AS POTHOLES BEAT CORTÈGE

A funeral cortège dropped mourners off two streets from their homes because of the state of a road near Bishop Auckland. The procession was taking no chances – one of the funeral cars had already broken a spring negotiating the lunar landscape of Dale Street, St Helens, on the way to the cemetery.

Local people are once again complaining that the road should be improved – but without much hope.

Examiner Lester Hind and his neighbours in adjoining Musgrave Street have manually drained the road in front of their terrace houses and built a dam of dirt and bricks to hold back the water.

'The water was two feet here', said Mr Hind, looking out over his front gate. 'I always carry a bucket and spade with me in the car to get out of the street. The only way to walk out is to leave by the back door and hug the wall of the houses across the back lane'.

He said he was frightened to let his partially sighted wife try to negotiate the pitted and puddled street on her own. Neighbour Wilf Shaw's wife is totally blind and because of the worsening condition of the street, she has not been out of doors for nine months. 'The council only acts when we have absolute floods', said Mr Shaw. And Mr Hind joined in: 'They'll come out after this piece appears in the *Northern Echo*. Then they'll forget about us.'

Northern Echo, 8 January 1976

Vogues of 1978. Joseph's technicolour dreamcoat has nothing on this outfit. It is as eye-catching as the model, which is saying something. (From *Northern Echo*, 6 June 1978)

Vogues of 1978. This hotch-potch of a collection looks as though it will be readily available in most Oxfam outlets, car boot and jumble sales. (From *Northern Echo*, 6 June 1978)

The stand-ins for 'brokers-men', the Krankies, in *Cinderella* at the Civic Theatre, Darlington, were Second Generation dancers Andy Rothwell and Chris Baldock.

KRANKIES BEAT THE SNOW TO GO ON WITH THE SHOW

Panto stars Ian and Jeanette Tough, alias the Krankies, adlibbed their way back into the show yesterday – ten minutes late after beating the snow drifts that had threatened to stop them appearing on national TV.

The couple, who found instant fame after appearing in the Royal Variety Performance, are in Cinderella at Darlington Civic theatre. And they were booked by the BBC to take part in the midnight Hogmanay party live from Glasgow on New Year's Eve, their Sunday night off from the panto.

They intended to drive to Glasgow after the curtain came down at 10 p.m. on Saturday. But all roads between the North-East and Scotland were blocked. On Sunday the BBC sent a light aircraft to pick them up at Teesside airport. The return flight, yesterday, was interrupted by a half-hour forced stop at Newcastle airport because visibility was down to 100 yards at Teesside. And during the wait they were questioned by police – because the pilot's girlfriend, along for the ride, had a Belfast accent!

Northern Echo, 2 January 1979

Opposite: This sixteenth-century well, discovered on the site of Darlington's £5 million recreation centre, opened another door into our fascinating past. Denis Coggin, antiquities officer at Bowes Museum, who examined the site, said: 'We found some fragments of sixteenth-century pottery, so it [the well], was probably built around that time. In those days any houses of consequence had a well.' How he would have drooled over the 260 million-year-old fossils found at Middridge Quarry, Newton Aycliffe.

RUBBISH TIP THREAT TO RARE FOSSIL FINDS

Fossils 260 million years old are in danger of being lost forever – under skip loads of rubbish.

Two-foot long fossilised fish – dating back to the days when the sea stretched from the Pennines to Germany – have been among the finds at Middridge Quarry, Newton Aycliffe. But now the quarry's owner plans to fill it with rubbish.

'Fossils are not much good to me,' said Darlington-based skip hirer Dave Ward. 'All I want to do is tip waste.' But his plans have brought protests from as far away as Reading. Yesterday a letter from the University there was received by Sedgefield District Council development control sub-committee, urging safeguards for an outcrop of rare marle slate.

Councillors also received a letter from Mr Tim Pettigrew, assistant keeper of natural sciences for Tyne and Wear Council. He described the site as outstanding, 'providing the first opportunity for nearly 100 years to collect a remarkable variety of plant and animal fossils – many of them rare.' He said a lot of the fossils could be found nowhere else. These particular rocks are only found in this country, in the North-East.

Northern Echo, 30 June 1978

In a letter to his employees, together with a statement of closure of Scotswood, Noel Davies, joint managing director of Vickers Engineering Group, said that the decision to shut the works down was reached only after 'a great deal of anguished thought'. This picture shows a Vickers yard in 1963.

ERA ENDS WITH 750 JOBS – DISBELIEF AS WELL AS DISMAY

There was dismay and almost disbelief on Tyneside last night, at the decision by Vickers, one of the most famous names in British Engineering, to close its Scotswood works.

Dismay because it means the loss of 758 jobs in an area with unemployment well above the national average; and disbelief because, although its troubles were well known, the closure has been announced by a firm 'synonymous with Tyneside for many lifetimes', as a top union man put it. Walkers Naval Yard, pictured, was not affected. Other Vickers factories on Tyneside were not affected. Next door to the doomed plant is Michell Bearings, with 500 jobs: a mile away, still in Scotswood Road, Elswick Works employ 1,191 and Crabtree Vickers in Gateshead has 402 workers.

The firm said that if short term measures were taken to save Scotswood, other businesses where jobs are now secure would be jeopardised.

Northern Echo, 6 January 1979

In March 1981 Billy Elliott, Darlington's boss, knew that the forthcoming match against bottom of the league Hereford would not be a pushover. This return of Sunday soccer to Feethams would test Darlington to the limit. If the team repeated its 3–0 defeat at Hartlepool on Boxing Day 1980, pictured here, Billy Elliott would be a happy man.

STRUGGLERS WILL TEST QUAKERS

Sunday soccer returns to Feethams tomorrow when Darlington try to check bottom of the league Hereford's explosive revival. After struggling in the re-election zone all season, Hereford have burst into life with convincing wins over Hartlepool and second division Shrewsbury in the last week.

Hartlepool's promotion hopes took a nasty blow with last Saturday's 3–0 defeat and Shrewsbury were swept aside 5–0 in a shock Welsh Cup result in midweek. One of the men behind the sudden recovery is former Middlesbrough and Carlisle striker Joe Laidlaw. A seasoned veteran who has played in all four divisions, he left Portsmouth in a £15,000 deal. Along with several other signings, he has brought hope to a club that could pull off a late surge to safety.

'They are going to be full of fight and confidence after those results and it is going to be tough for us,' said Darlington boss, Billy Elliott. 'It is up to us to show how much we want to win. If there's the slightest complacency we'll be in trouble.'

Elliott sticks to the team that could have played in last week's postponed game against Port Vale. Harry Charlton plays his first full game for a couple of months and Roger Wicks continues a substitute.

Darlington: Cuff, Kamara, McLean, Ball, Skipper, Smith, Speedie, Charlton, Stalker, Hamilton, Walsh, Sub. Wicks.

Northern Echo, 7 March 1981

After what must have been hours of anguished thought, a scholar pronounced that two sexes are best. This picture shows some happy diners, all of whom would not have it any other way. What a pity highly paid academics have nothing better to do than pontificate on such frivolous matters.

TWO SEXES ARE BEST . . . OFFICIAL

A Durham academic has come to the conclusion that the existence of two sexes is a very good idea. 'Three sexes wouldn't work', says university 'expert', Dr Paul Greenwood. 'And though we could all be the same, research shows this would not be nearly so interesting.'

The doctor, a zoologist, also thinks it very sensible for there to be roughly equal numbers of men and women in the world. 'Any other arrangement makes no sense at all,' he said yesterday.

Dr Greenwood aims to give people a proper understanding of the birds and the bees during an adult education course lasting 16 weeks.

He and sociologist Sheila Cross will also deal a few blows to male chauvinists.

'For starters,' said Dr Greenwood, 'females are often larger than males – and the human male is more likely to die.

'I find that people come out with the most outrageous statements concerning allegedly innate differences between men and women,' he said. 'We are starting with the biological viewpoint before going on to consider alternative explanations for the sex roles in society.'

Northern Echo, 17 September 1981

This picture of one of the workshops in Durham jail gives no hint of the overcrowding then causing concern in the prison.

RIOT KIDS HIT JAIL FLASHPOINT

Street rioters have bought a new wave of trouble to the overcrowded Durham Jail.

The number of offences by inmates last year was revealed yesterday to be 700, and prison officers said that newly jailed rioters had now started assaulting staff and defying the entire regime.

'These young people are brought in for rioting, and it is continuing in here. There are more and more cases showing up daily,' said a leading member of Durham Prison Officers' Association.

On the Home Office figures for last year, he commented, 'We could get that many every day if we felt like it. It's got to the stage where we only take up the serious cases.'

A large proportion of incidents involve insubordination.

The officer added, 'Prisoners used to accept the consequences of their crimes, but this element of young people no longer accepts the regime. They just slouch about.'

Officers pin a lot of the blame for the high figures on overcrowding. Durham had an average population of 931 men last year. The official limit is 650.

However, [a] former inmate, who is now writing a book about prisons, said, 'Some Durham officers provoked and baited prisoners.'

Northern Echo, 10 October 1981

The
Progressive Years

Margaret Thatcher, Britain's first lady Prime Minister, was making a profound impression in the House of Commons. She was a formidable politician with the makings of an outstanding prime minister – just what the country needed. Love her or hate her we could not ignore her. Already she was a giant among so many pigmy politicians.

THIS JOB IS A NIGHTMARE SAYS MAGGIE

Running Britain gives Mrs Thatcher nightmares and many sleepless hours, she admitted on the eve of her toughest Tory Party conference.

Britain's first woman Prime Minister said, 'If there's something very worrying coming up the next day and you might have worked on a speech until 3.30 in the morning . . . you go to bed eventually. You close your eyes and everything goes round and round.

'You get a dream, not a very nice one – connected with everything you've been thinking about,' she told *Woman's Own* magazine.

Northern Echo, 19 October 1981

Darlington was never a walled town, so The Hole in the Wall, pictured here, was not named for that reason. It is an old pub without frills. It was not a place where the elite met to eat; but times they were a-changing.

LEAVE OUR LOCAL ALONE! HOLE IN THE WALL GANG SNIFFS AT PANCAKE PLAN

The minute you walk in the joint you can see it's a pub of distinction. No thick-pile carpets, piped music or cosy seats here. No exotic cocktails and definitely no fancy bar meals. But it is distinctive.

As boozers go, it's basic – and that's exactly how drinkers in the Hole in the Wall in Darlington market place want their local to stay. They are outraged at plans by Imperial Inns and Taverns to give the 100-year-old pub a bright new look.

The company intends to give the pub a new name. Out will go the fruit machine, jukebox and pool table and in their place will come stereo sound and Darlington's first creperie, selling French-style pancakes.

'What the hell's a creperie?', asked one drinker yesterday lunchtime as he supped his pint in the corner of the pub's only bar. When told, he said, 'You must be joking – pancakes in a pub!'

Oil rig worker Bill Tait, a regular for three years, said, 'they are destroying the pubs. This is a nice friendly boozer with lots of atmosphere.

'If they spend thousands making it all posh it will destroy the character.' . . .

Northern Echo, 1 September 1984

Opposite: In the 1920s the Turkey Trot was all the rage. Today it is Loftus Turkey Run that attracts many male athletes, as this picture shows. But in a women-only road race there was something odd about one of the runners – a five o'clock shadow!

THE LADY RUNNER WITH THE FIVE O'CLOCK SHADOW

There was something odd about one of the competitors among thousands that took part in a women-only road run at the weekend. Certain bumps were in the right place and there was even a smart handbag dangling from the right wrist. But was that a trace of stubble on the chin? And those muscular, hairy arms and legs prompted comment. The truth came out at the end when Peter Galloway emerged from his dress, wig and heavy make-up.

He had managed to be the only man to take part in the nationwide event when he ran the *Woman's Own* Nike Six Mile run. The run, organised by the magazine to encourage fitness among its readers and raise money for Save the Children's Bone Marrow Unit Appeal, was held in 3 different towns. Peter's wife Colette entered the Darlington run to raise funds for Middleton St George Play Group but was pushed too hard on training by her coach – Peter – and damaged her ankle. 'We didn't want to lose all the money we'd been promised in sponsorship so there was nothing else for it. I agreed to run in her place even if it meant dressing up,' said Peter, a 33-year-old squash player, who says it was his first run. Organisers threatened to disqualify him at the start but relented when they realised his intention was not to make a mockery of an all-women event but was for a good cause. He finished in 67 minutes 42 seconds.

Northern Echo, 3 September 1984

Celebrating the seventy-fifth anniversary of the Civic Theatre on 2 September 1982 are Ken Dodd and William MacDonald, the theatre's director. The special anniversary was marked by a gala performance by Ken Dodd and was attended by the Mayor and Mayoress of Darlington, Councillor and Mrs William Newton.

Entertaining Mr Sloane, one of the plays presented in the Civic's spring 1985 programme. Back: Peter Adamson and Frank Gatliff; front: Christopher Fulford and Pamela Sholto.

The celebrated entertainer Roy Hudd loves playing the Civic, Darlington, 'a real Edwardian theatre'. He is an authority on traditional old-time music hall and an enthusiastic collector of music hall song sheets.

No Tune Like an Old Tune

Comedian Roy Hudd likes nothing better than browsing among his collection of 10,000 old music hall song sheets. And it was during these leisure spells that he got the idea for a show that is delighting audiences up and down the country.

'Just A Verse And Chorus' this week features the work of two prolific writers Bob Weston and Bert Lee.

Roy, who stars in the show with Billy Dainty, said yesterday, 'So little is really known about these two that we have to tailor the personalities to ourselves. They turned out over 3,000 songs along during the early part of the century and 90 per cent of them were first class.

'Their work was used by many of the stars of the day including Sunderland's Wee Georgie Wood, Stanley Holloway, Gracie Fields and Rob Wilton. In their heyday, Weston and Lee, who died before the end of the last war, turned out a song a day, apart from writing sketches and pantomime. It is said that many a time they posted songs to their publishers without even playing them over,' said Roy. 'They reckoned they could hear what they sounded like.'

Northern Echo, 2 October 1985

North-Eastern people have always given generously to good causes, including relief for the starving in places like Ethiopia, pictured here. Sometimes the organisers hit snags.

BAND AID LET US DOWN, SAYS DAVE

Charity concert organiser, Dave Birdsall, was down in the dumps yesterday when nobody from the London-based Band Aid turned up in Cleveland to collect a cheque for £6,000 towards the starving in Africa.

Most of the money had been raised at a concert at Thornaby's Teesside Park on September 21st where groups of dancers and singers performed free.

Dave, 23, of Roseworth, said he had been promised by a London official from the charity that a member would arrive at Middlesbrough Town Hall to accept the cheque. But although television and newsmen waited to report the event, Dave could only say he had been bitterly let down. He said Band Aid's attitude was 'one hell of a snub' and took the cheque home to post.

'The people of Cleveland have been slapped in the face, having given so generously. It would appear the super stars who played in the Wembly concert only did it to boost their careers and we in the North do not matter,' he said. But last night a spokesman for Band Aid in London said they were 'profusely sorry' for not being present and in no way did they intend to snub Cleveland. 'We send our heartfelt thanks and shall be speaking to Mr Birdsall to apologise in person,' said press officer Bernard Doherty.

Northern Echo, 4 October 1985

A Changing
Environment

A male mallard shows he is 'quackers' about David Bellamy who, for so many years has done outstanding work to improve the environment.

FIRST AID FOR VILLAGE

David Bellamy joined a host of school children yesterday to launch the North-East's first branch of a national environment organisation.

The TV botanist and Durham University professor was in Peterlee to mark the official opening of the East Durham Groundwork Trust.

Young fun runners and Groundwork Foundation chairman Chris Chataway put their best foot forward to give the Trust a racing start at Peterlee Leisure Centre. The East Durham Trust is one of a dozen Groundwork groups nationwide dedicated to caring for an improving environment.

The Trust's headquarters are in Thornaby Station Industrial Estate, Shotton Colliery.

Northern Echo, 19 May 1987

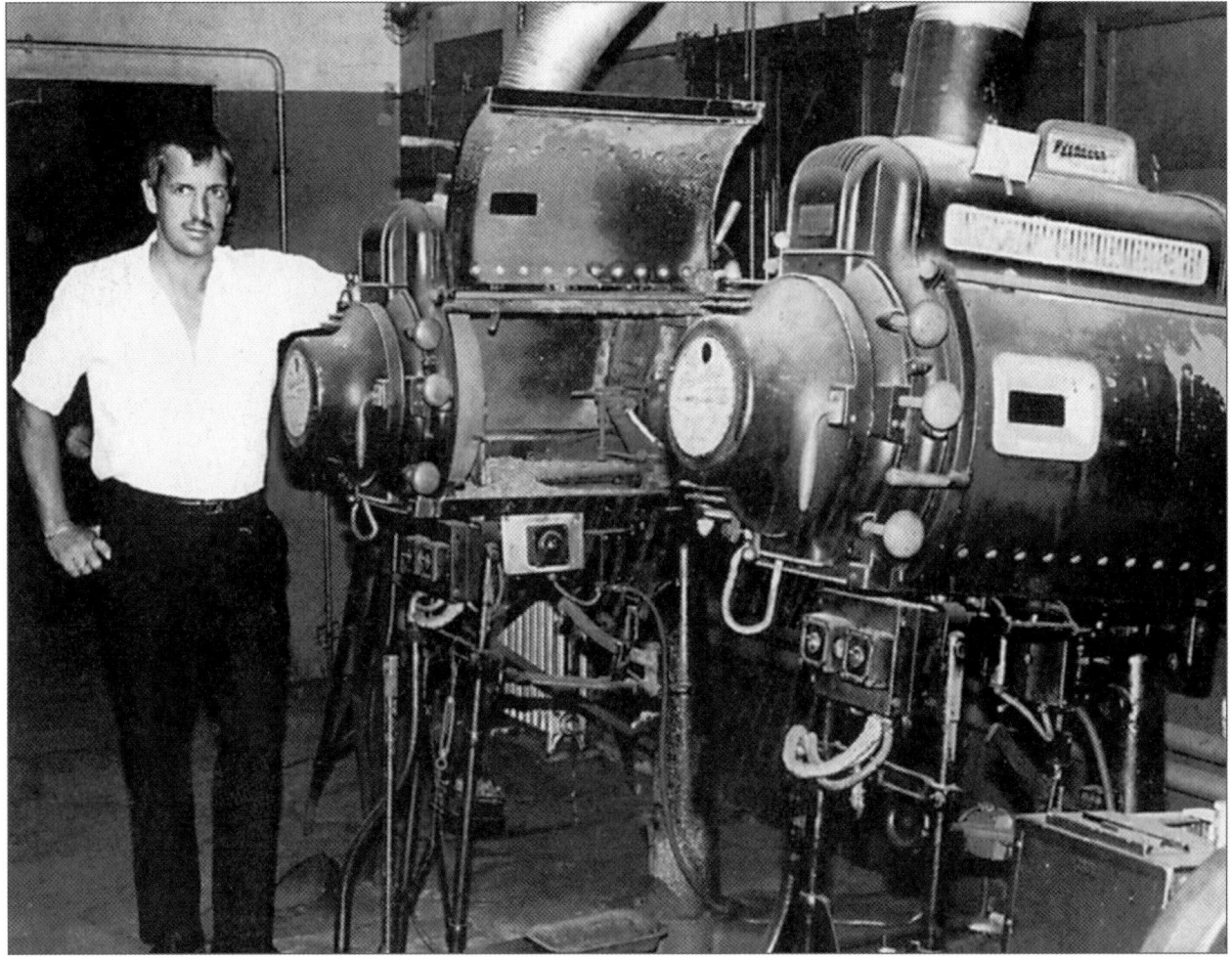

The Regent cinema in Cobden Street opened in 1939. It moved with the times and was later equipped with stereophonic sound. Duncan Bannatyne stands by the projectors, 1987.

VANDALS PLOUGH UP GOLF COURSE

Vandals have wrecked a Darlington golf course by ploughing up the green and carving the message 'hello'.

And yesterday head greenkeeper, Michael Lawson, said, 'I am devastated by what's happened. It's so soul destroying.'

A Darlington police spokesman said the attack – the latest of several – happened at the town's Stressholme Golf Club on Wednesday night and caused about £1,000 worth of damage.

Mr Lawson told yesterday how the green was all ready for a home and away game against Middlesbrough Municipal on Saturday. It had just been repaired after another vandal attack three weeks ago.

Now club members and staff are working round the clock to patch up the ruined area – about a third of the whole course – in time for Saturday's tournament.

'It's my pride and joy. I like to see it looking nice,' said Mr Lawson, who was alerted of the damage by a club member at about 7.15 a.m. yesterday. 'Two of us have been working at it, but it still isn't right.'

And a club member, who did not want to be named, said, 'Tempers are running very high here at the moment. It has happened many times, but this is the worst attack. The head greenkeeper is absolutely devastated.'

Northern Echo, 1 September 1987

On the right track for discovering 'the last undiscovered dale', seen here in 1974.

MORE TAKE THE LINE TO WEARDALE

Almost double the amount of passengers used an experimental rail service into a burgeoning tourist area this summer.

A survey still being carried out by Durham County Council shows that on average 150 people used the Heritage Line rail service between Bishop Auckland and Stanhope each Sunday this summer.

In its inaugural year, last year, the figure was just 80.

The line, which has the backing of a group of local authorities, is aimed at bringing tourists into Weardale. Wear Valley District Council Labour Leader Coun John Richardson said, 'It justifies the work that we have been doing.' He said he felt the line had an extremely important role to play in the attraction of tourists. 'We have always said that Weardale was the last undiscovered dale.'

Northern Echo, 8 September 1989

Explorer Robert Swan received a wonderful homecoming following his return from the Arctic.

TRIBUTES TO ICE WALKER

Family and friends gathered yesterday for a service of thanksgiving for the safe return from the Arctic of icewalk leader Robert Swan, the only man to have walked to both Poles.

Darlington-born Robert, currently on a world-wide tour, attended the service at St Mary's Church, Wycliffe, near Barnard Castle, with his mother, Margaret who lives in the village.

There was a break with protocol during the service when the congregation joined in loud applause for his achievements.

Speaking on behalf of the parish, churchwarden Eddie Pooley recalled how his previous welcome home speech from the Antarctic had been tinged with sadness at the sinking of the expedition's supply ship.

'Robert did not walk away from his problems. He set about repaying massive debts before embarking on his Arctic trek. He is a great example.'

Northern Echo, 11 September 1989

Members of the 7th Battalion, The Durham Light Infantry, pictured here sounding the retreat at Hartlepool's Historic Quay, know how to treat our glorious dead – with all due respect. It would be fitting for them to knock some respect into the lager louts who desecrate our war memorials – and do it the hard way.

TOWN WAR MEMORIALS DESECRATED

Old soldiers have launched a fierce attack on 'lager louts' who, they claim, are desecrating a town's war memorials.

Two ex-servicemen's associations have branded the youngsters' antics as sacrilege. And they are urging Hartlepool Council to take action to combat the problem.

Honorary secretary of the Hartlepool branch of the Dunkirk Veterans Assocations, Arthur Uden, said members were concerned about the state of the war memorials in Victoria Road and on the Headland.

'These are being frequented by hooligans and lager louts who dispose of their litter and empty cans around the base of the memorials. Some are even writing graffiti on the memorials.'

Mr Uden added, 'We ex-servicemen who served in the last war and many others of the older generation who remember the horrors of the conflict consider that these memorials – erected and dedicated in honour of these men and women, who gave their lives in the cause of freedom – should be treated with the respect they deserve.'

The local branch of the Durham Light Infantry Association says youths climb and urinate on the memorials.

'Please try and do something as this is absolute sacrilege,' says a letter to the council.

The matter will be discussed by the recreation sub-committee this afternoon.

'Although we are taking action to try and resolve some of the problems, this may take some time, particularly the pursuing of a by-law to prevent drinking in public places,' said director of leisure services Clive Addison.

Northern Echo, 2 October 1989

Darlington, seen here in the 1930s, played a major part in the opening of the first public railway worked by steam on 27 September 1825 and set the pattern for the development of the railway system throughout the world. On 1 January 1870 the *Northern Echo* was first printed and quickly gained a formidable reputation for, in the words of its most famous editor W.T. Stead, 'attacking the devil'. Darlington is also home to very important firms like Whessoe Ltd, supplier of plant to the nuclear power, gas and oil industries, Cleveland Bridge, builder of major bridges throughout the world, and Paton and Baldwins, the wool people, among others. Its magical Edwardian theatre, the Civic, is probably the most successful provincial theatre in the country; and the town has produced its full share of outstanding citizens. It has a (sometimes) creditable football team – the Quakers – as well as a cricket team, golf and other athletic facilities. Yet movie mogul David Puttnam had the temerity to call it 'just another town' in 1989. When Darlington Mayor Barrie Lamb wrote to him about his remarks the letter remained unanswered.

MOVIE MAKER FAILS TO WRITE

Darlington Mayor Barrie Lamb is still waiting to hear from movie mogul David Puttnam, whose comments about the town sparked fury nearly a month ago. Mr Puttnam promised to write to Coun. Lamb after labelling Darlington 'just another town' in a speech in Bristol.

His remarks brought furious reaction from Coun. Lamb, Darlington's MP Michael Fallon and Civic Theatre boss Brian Goddard.

Yesterday Coun. Lamb said, 'We've heard nothing. He knows my name and the address of the town hall. But he has not been in touch.'

Northern Echo, 4 October 1989

The Bishop of Durham would not be the Bishop of Durham if he were not controversial.

MESSAGE FOR CHRISTMAS CONTROVERSY

The Bishop of Durham started another storm yesterday as he gave a sermon from the pulpit of a North-East church. Around one million listeners heard the controversial sermon broadcast on radio from the pulpit of St Peter's Church, Stockton, as the Rt Revd David Jenkins talked of poverty, consumption, exploitation and greed.

He went on to criticise the way in which Christmas had become privatised and commercialised.

While several politicians called on the Bishop to resign, St Peter's new vicar, Revd Alex Whitehead, said the Bishop had only preached the basic gospel.

'If anyone finds that controversial it means they have missed the basic point of the Christian faith,' he said.

The Bishop said people had been forced out of a cash-based society by being made redundant.

He said . . . 'Consumption, exploitation and greed are using up the earth in the direction of destruction while at the same time many starve. The practical touchstone will be whether or not the poor are hearing the good news and this will be connected with whether Jesus is quietly domesticated in some privatised and commercialised Christmas for prosperous families or whether he emerges as a disturbance and a likely stumbling block'.

Stockton Tory councillor Stephen Smalles asked, 'Where is this poverty in the North? I have never seen poverty in this town. Let him resign, give up his seat in the House of Lords and try to win one in the House of Commons. Politics should not be preached from the pulpit'.

Northern Echo, 15 December 1989

Darlington's bus users were spoiled for choice during the town's bus war, which Stagecoach was odds-on favourite to win. Clifton Road, pictured here, was part of the battlefield.

BUS BOSS REJECTS WAR TALK CLAIMING RESIDENTS DEMANDED NEW SERVICE

The battle ground for Darlington's bus war is set to move to Skerne Park. Newcomer firm Your Bus launches a service to the estate on August 18, leaving the town centre six times an hour on the same route as rival United.

But six weeks after residents at Springwell Terrace campaigned to keep waves of buses out, fears are growing that Clifton Road could be the next danger spot.

Your Bus managing director Andrew Guest said last night, 'We have had a lot of requests from people in Skerne Park asking if we are extending our service from Whinbush through to there.'

He said the routes have come about through reorganisation rather than new investment and would mean fewer buses going to Whinbush.

Skerne Park resident Joyce Standing welcomed more buses but warned, 'A lot of children play on the street and we do not want any of the carry-on they have over at Haughton.'

Northern Echo, 20 July 1993

Among the reasons given for train delays have been leaves on the line and the wrong kind of snow. This could be the latest excuse – lost contact with a satellite.

THE TRAIN LEAVING PLATFORM SIX IS TRACKED BY SATELLITE

It may have been equipped with the latest in US Defence Dept satellites – but the 10.25 Dundee to Penzance was still six minutes late into Darlington.

The delay may have been due to the launch of Intercity's new carriages. Their arrival attracted a train load of reporters, camera crews and photographers.

Passengers enjoying a quiet trip to the South were bombarded with questions and asked to pose for pictures as the train sped along at 125 mph.

Intercity has spent thousands developing two carriages in its fleet of 1,300 and invited the world's assorted media to show the public just what could be done if the ready cash was available.

Computerised passenger information displays calculated from information beamed from satellites orbiting 11,000 miles away from earth form part of the package.

The GPS equipment computes the exact position of the train from a network of 21 satellites and automatically updates the on-board displays as the journey progresses.

Fancy washrooms, extra baggage space and new carpets have also been fitted, while customers have the chance to tune in to the latest sounds via an onboard entertainment channel featuring CDs and radio.

For just £2 the happy traveller can buy a headphone set from the buffet.

'It is all very comfortable and really gets you in the holiday spirit,' said passenger Anthony Delahoy from Edinburgh.

Northern Echo, 7 September 1993

Good news on the ornithological front. Birds of prey were on the increase in the North-East, strengthening the delicate balance of nature. They are, without exception, magnificent creatures.

NORTH-EAST KINDEST PLACE FOR BIRDS OF PREY

Birds of prey in the North-East are being given a better chance of survival than their cousins elsewhere in the country, according to bird lovers.

A new report by the Royal Society for the Protection of Birds shows a 20 per cent increase in crime against all birds nationwide – the largest increase being in the persecution of birds of prey.

But in the North-East, birds of prey are getting a better deal, RSPB regional spokesman David Hirst said last night.

Mr Hirst said, 'Illegal poisoning, shooting and trapping of birds of prey still continues, but a very small number of people are involved. 'People in the region realise that we all have an interst in protecting the species.' Mr Hirst said good management of heather and moorland seen in the Yorkshire Dales was important for all wild life.

He added, 'The continued colonisation of these areas by birds of prey is very welcome. From strongholds there, they will eventually move elsewhere, re-colonising other areas of the North-East.'

Mr Hirst added incidents of wanton vandalism still posed a serious threat to other species in the region. He said prime concerns included shooting of swans and ducks.

Other remaining problems were the theft of birds' eggs from nests by obsessive collectors and illegal falconry crimes.

Northern Echo, 7 December 1993

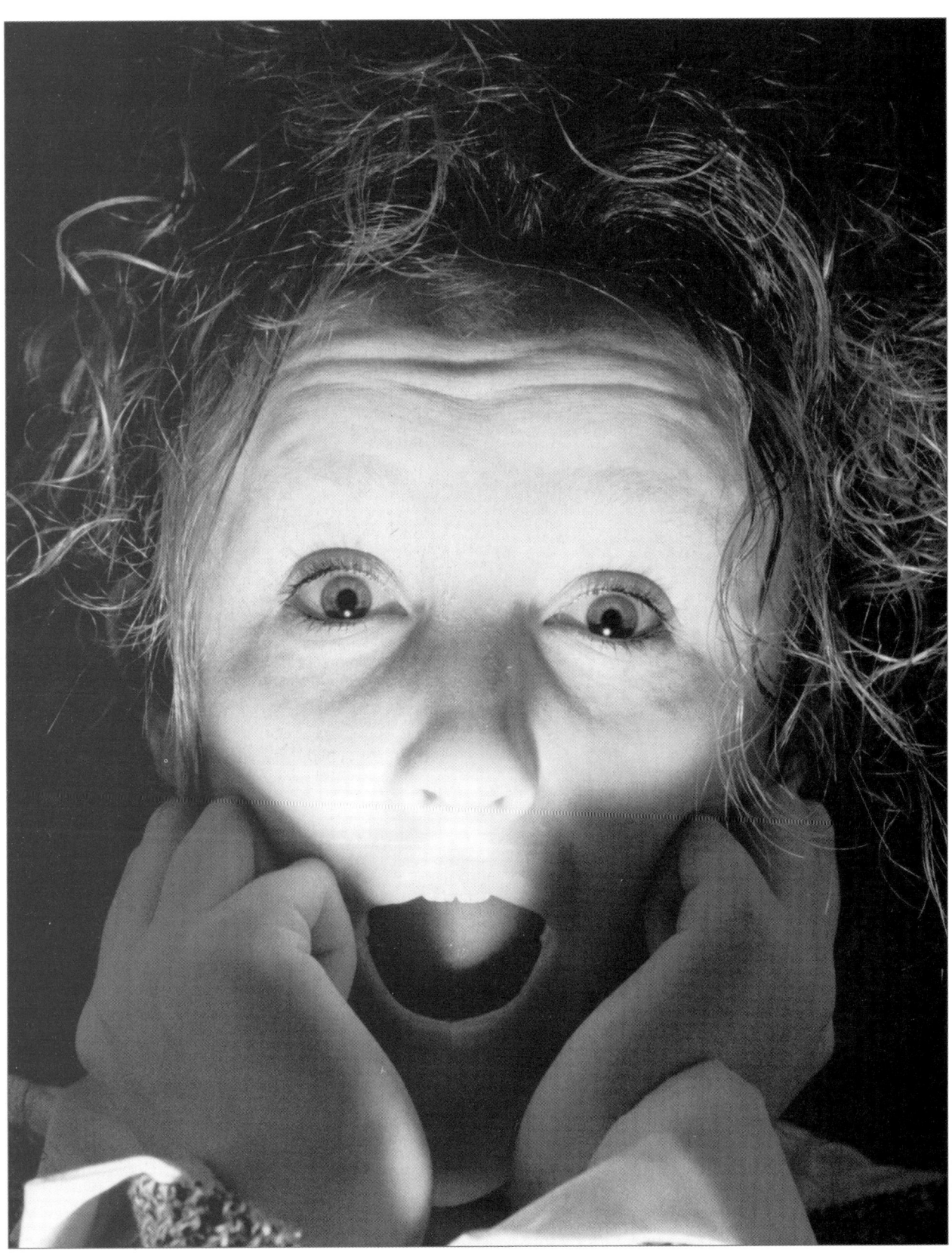

The railway pioneer Timothy Hackworth, whose bust is pictured here, resided in Soho House, new Shildon, from 1833 until 1850. He was never happier than acting as host in the house he called Soho Cottage. It is now the Timothy Hackworth Museum.

THIEVES STRIKE AGAIN AT MUSEUM

A museum has been hit by a third burglary during its 21st anniversary year. Theieves took an antique clock, valued at several hundred pounds in the latest raid on the Timothy Hackworth Victorian Railway Museum in Shildon.

Security has been stepped up at the heritage centre which attracts about 12,000 visitors a year after the third raid in eight months.

A writing box, which belonged to the family of North-East railway pioneer Timothy Hackworth was stolen earlier in the summer.

The thefts have particularly upset staff because many of the items in its historic displays were donated by local people.

Northern Echo, 5 September 1996

Opposite: Since all pubs serve spirits they can be expected to be the haunt of phantoms. Arrgh! Sorry I spook!

PUB GHOUL TAKES TWO KEENAN INTEREST

Ghoulish goings on are spooking customers at a pub.

The ghost is believed to be the spirit of a Canadian airman and, in a strange twist to the story, his latest victim shares the same surname as the previous one. Stephanie Keenan, from Marske, East Cleveland, jumped out of her skin after finishing a meal at the Golden Fleece pub in Pavement, York, and spotting an old man in a dirty mac sitting next to her. But a closer look revealed that nobody was there and the barman then revealed the strange tale of an American tourist, April Keenan.

She was staying in the pub over Easter last year when the cheeky dead airman apparently pulled her hair and touched her feet and arms.

It is thought that the ghost is the spirit of a Canadian flier who hanged himself at the pub.

Landlady Sally Pyne said, 'To have it happen to a person of the same name at the same time of year is totally bizarre.'

Stephanie said, 'All I could see was a man in a waxy mac sitting next to me. I am all right now, but I was a bit scared afterwards. I woke up at 3 a.m. and I had to switch the light on.'

Northern Echo, 24 April 1995

The *Northern Echo* and leaders of industry alerted Prime Minister Tony Blair to serious economic problems in the North-East because of a strong pound.

WE'RE HURTING, PRIME MINISTER

The Government came under pressure last night to take immediate action to stem the tide of job losses in the North-East. The *Northern Echo* will today send an open letter to Prime Minister, Tony Blair, urging him to persuade the Bank of England to cut interest rates and lower the value of the pound to relieve the pressure on manufacturers and exporters.

The letter is supported by leaders of the business community and trade unions in the region.

It follows the latest body blow to the North-East economy yesterday, when crane-maker Grove Worldwide announced the closure of its factory in Sunderland with the loss of 670 jobs.

Dear Mr Blair,

By the time you come back from your summer holiday, thousands of people in the North-East will have lost their jobs or will face the real threat of unemployment. Most of them voted for your party at the General Election in the hope that you would look after their interests. Some of them are in your Sedgefield constituency. On behalf of our region, the *Northern Echo* asks you to take urgent action to stem the tide of job losses which threatens to plunge the region into a recession as severe as it has ever witnessed.

The jobs disappearing or in jeopardy are not in the traditional heavy industries which were once the mainstay of the regional economy. They are all showpiece inward investors, at the leading edge of modern technology. They are the new jobs on which the North-East's much vaunted economic survival is based. Our region remains heavily dependent on manufacturing and exports. As such we are bearing the brunt of the effect of the high interest rates and strong pound brought on by your Government's economic policy.

continued opposite

Tups like this magnificent Swaledale shearling are a regular feature of Wolsingham Agricultural Show.

220th agricultural show is a winner as seven-year-old attendance record falls. 30,000 flocked to the big shows. Organisers are celebrating what they believe to be a record weekend at Weardale's biggest agricultural show. The 220th Annual Wolsingham Agricultural Show is thought to have broken the record of 31,000 visitors set in 1991.

Northern Echo, 7 September 1998

continued from p. 122
   The workforce of our region is among the most productive and adaptable in Europe. We have recovered from collapse of traditional industries like coal mining and ship building by a formidable combination of endeavour, enterprise and flexibility. Now we are suffering because the strong pound is making our products less competitive abroad. It is time for you to act, to bring down interest rates and allow the pound to reach more competitive and realistic levels.
   We are not asking for preferential treatment, simply a level economic playing field with our competitor regions in the UK and Europe. On that basis we are confident the North-East will be able to shrug aside the current hardships and emerge as an even stronger industrial fighting force.

Colin Topping, *Northern Echo*
Michael Bird, Chief Executive, North-East Chamber of Commerce
Arthur Foord, Regional Director, Confederation of British Industry
Bob Howard Regional Secretary, TUC

Northern Echo, 11 August 1998

The new millennium dawned on a high for the people of Great Britain. Our constitutional monarchy, with Queen Elizabeth II at its head, is still the envy of many other countries. Our form of democratic government is not perfect – no form of government is – but our version of it is second to none, which gives us cause to count our blessings and be thankful.

Acknowledgements & Picture Credits

First and foremost my special thanks go to David Kelly, managing director of the *Northern Echo*, and to Peter Barron, editor of this great newspaper, for allowing me the privilege of exploring the paper's archives, a most enjoyable occupation. Thank you Eagle Graphics for the typing. What a pleasure it is being part of Sutton Publishing's brilliant team: Simon Fletcher, Anne Bennett, Sarah Moore, Michelle Tilling and Joyce Percival. Heave ho! Away we go, all pulling together in the same direction; and it works. It is a good feeling, being in such talented company and among friends. Should you find any errors, dear reader, they belong to me. If I have overlooked anyone it is inadvertent and I apologise for this. All the pictures contained in this book are from the *Northern Echo*'s collection unless otherwise stated.